*Institutions observed: towards a new
concept of secure provision
in mental health*

King Edward's Hospital Fund for London

Patron: Her Majesty The Queen

President: HRH The Prince of Wales

Treasurer: Robin Dent
Chairman of the Management Committee: The Hon Hugh Astor JP
Secretary: Robert J Maxwell JP PhD

King Edward's Hospital Fund for London is an independent foundation, established in 1897 and incorporated by Act of Parliament 1907, and is a registered charity. It seeks to encourage good practice and innovation in the management of health care by research, experiment and education, and by direct grants.

Appeals for these purposes continue to increase.

The Treasurer would welcome any new sources of money, in the form of donations, deeds of covenant or legacies, which would enable the Fund to augment its activities.

Requests for the annual report, which includes a financial statement, lists of all grants and other information, should be addressed to the Secretary, King Edward's Hospital Fund for London, 14 Palace Court, London W2 4HT.

Institutions observed: towards a new concept of secure provision in mental health

Larry Gostin

King Edward's Hospital Fund for London

ISBN 0 19 724634 6

King's Fund Publishing Office
126 Albert Street
London NW1 7NF

Contents

Foreword

Larry Gostin is well known for his work at MIND and elsewhere as an informed campaigner for the mentally ill, including those held under compulsory orders or as a result of criminal conviction. The work that led to the present book was undertaken while he was on a year's sabbatical at the Centre for Criminological Research at Oxford University, and was partly financed by a grant from the King's Fund.

I recognise that the book will be controversial and suggest that it is none the worse for that. Larry Gostin is a careful, conscientious person. That does not mean that his conclusions are beyond argument or challenge, but that they are to be taken seriously. An early draft of the typescript was discussed at a meeting which I chaired at the King's Fund Centre in October 1984. It aroused much interest and some hostility, the main criticisms concentrating on the chapter about the special hospitals. I know that Larry Gostin listened carefully to all that was said and has since made many changes of detail to that chapter, although the results will no doubt still leave many of his critics dissatisfied. His conclusions are his own, not those of the King's Fund. What I am determined to defend is his right to reach his own conclusions in matters of such importance affecting individual welfare and liberty, and reflecting the values of society as a whole. What is more, I believe it is the King's Fund's duty to publish them however controversial they may be, knowing that they have been reached in good faith.

We have taken the unusual step of asking two people to comment on Larry's typescript and are publishing their comments as part of the book. We are grateful to Lord Colville of Culross, Chairman of the Mental Health Act Commission, and Dr T W Harding, a distinguished psychiatrist, for willingly undertaking this difficult task and to Larry Gostin for agreeing to it. Our purpose was to provide an element of balance to a radical and comprehensive review, which cannot be expected to be seen as fair by everybody.

In conclusion, may I say two things to anybody who finds the book one-sided. First, please hold any initial prejudice you may have in suspense and read carefully what Larry Gostin has written. Second, I believe there is special value in his having tried to see and present the whole subject of secure provision, rather than addressing a fragment of it. Incremental improvements, which are already being made in this difficult field, need to be fitted into a much broader, more comprehensive strategy.

Robert J Maxwell
Secretary
King Edward's Hospital Fund for London

Preface

Nothing touches the lives of mentally ill and mentally handicapped people more than the setting within which they are cared for and treated. The statutory basis for the current institutions which house mentally disordered people was derived from the County Asylums Act of 1808, and many institutions today are on the original sites. Even in those days, special kinds of madhouses were being built to confine the dangerous lunatic, with two buildings of the Bethlem Hospital being used for this special purpose. On 6 August 1860 an Act was passed for the better provision for the custody and care of criminal lunatics which resulted in the building of Broadmoor in 1863 with convict labour. In the early 20th century the other two special hospitals, Rampton (1910) and Moss Side (1914) were opened.

That was the beginning of our policy of designing specially secure institutions for dangerous mentally disordered people. The move towards 'separate institutions' for 'dangerous' and 'non-dangerous' patients emerged very clearly in the 1950s and 1960s with the development of the 'open-door' philosophy in local NHS hospitals. Mental illness was seen as akin to physical illness and local hospitals were designed to treat, not to confine, patients. This changed the whole nature of the mental health services. Local hospitals began to lose the capability of caring for difficult or dangerous patients, and would all too readily refuse to admit difficult patients – particularly mentally disordered offenders.

The open-door policy was a great advantage for most mentally disordered people, but caused intractable problems for a significant minority of 'less attractive' patients. Many mentally disordered people were sentenced to imprisonment because courts could not find more appropriate placements in local hospitals; and the special hospitals were overcrowded with patients who did not require maximum security conditions.

The government's response to this problem was to create yet more specialisation. Secure units were planned in each regional health authority in England, and in Wales. These regional secure units are now operational in many regions, and they have added another tier of security to the mental health services. At the same time, a great deal has been invested in the special hospitals, with the rebuilding and extension of Broadmoor and Rampton and the building of a new special hospital (Park Lane). This has occurred while the rest of the mental health services have suffered retrenchment, making it even less likely that local hospitals will be able to cope with the problems of managing difficult patients. Such massive capital spending on secure provision (which has gone hand-in-hand with the building of new prisons) has simply pre-empted an intelligent policy discussion as to what services really are needed.

The fact is that the policy of specialised secure conditions for 'dangerous' patients is based upon unfounded assumptions. We now know from voluminous research (see, for example, Bowden 1985), that 'dangerousness' is not such a clear and well-defined concept as was once thought. Mentally disordered people cannot be designated accurately as either 'dangerous all of the time' or 'dangerous none of the time'. 'Dangerousness' is not a constant, fixed personal charac-teristic. Rather, mentally disordered people may pose a risk at certain times and in response to certain situations but not in others; they are highly vulnerable complex human beings whose behaviour is often more disruptive than very dangerous.

The policy of 'separate institutions' has never been seriously ques-tioned. Indeed, we have failed to look at the evidence which has long been available about what today's institutions are doing to their populations – that evidence goes well beyond the inquiries which have uncovered maltreatment or neglect. Once in a particular kind of specialised institution, the patient is powerfully affected. Those in secure hospitals like Broadmoor have remained there for years, many for a lifetime. Conditions in the special hospitals are highly restrictive, sometimes punitive, and when patients are transferred or discharged they have the indelible stigma of having been a 'special' patient. In many ways, admission to a secure institution is a self-fulfilling prophecy; patients come to be regarded as dangerous, otherwise why would they be there?

This book seeks to document the harm caused by secure institu-tions. It also tries to jolt policy makers into the realisation that a debate and a search for alternative models of care are now necessary. If we are to continue to have institutions (and the fact is that we are likely to have them for as long as they have been in existence already) we have to make them flexible enough to meet the diverse needs of their inhabitants.

I try to make the case for 'flexible' institutions in these pages, meaning that staff in local hospitals and residential accommodation should have the resources to deal with periodic outbursts of difficult or dangerous behaviour without needing to transfer the patient to a secure institution. This would require better facilities to contain difficult patients and more well-trained staff to carry out the containment sensitively and less obtrusively. Local hospitals should be able to control or remove a patient during a violent episode, and to return the patient to more open and normal conditions once the risk has passed. The intention is to make it very much less necessary to place mentally disordered people in prisons or secure mental hospitals.

We have for too long cavalierly assumed that old institutions and policies actually benefit people, when often they do not. Many of my proposals may not provide the right answers, but it is incumbent on the government and mental health professionals to begin to consider the problems and to put forward their own ideas for the reform of institutions which badly need to be changed.

Acknowledgements

I am indebted to the King Edward's Hospital Fund for London for the generous support they have given to this project, and particularly Robert Maxwell, Tom McAusland, David Towell and Victor Morrison. The King's Fund hosted a high level policy conference on a draft copy of this report attended principally by providers of secure services. The day was charged with controversy – and so it should have been because thinking about change is never easy. It is to the service providers that we shall have to look for response to ideas from the 'outside'; and it is for them to blend these ideas with their own invaluable experience and personal know-how. I want to thank a number of professionals who have given me access to their institutions and their ideas in an open spirit, particularly Sir Leslie Teeman and Dr Alf Minto, who spent an entire day showing Robert Maxwell and myself around Rampton. I also wish to thank MIND, notably Chris Heginbotham and William Bingley, for all their considerable help.

The King's Fund Secure Provision project was housed in the Oxford University Centre for Criminological Research, and I want to acknowledge the kindness and help of Roger Hood and Andrew Ashworth. The King's Fund project resulted in a series of essays I edited, which complement this report: *Secure provision: a review of special services for the mentally ill and mentally handicapped in England and Wales* (London, Tavistock Publications 1985). That publication provides the factual background for understanding secure provision, much of which is not repeated in this report.

Larry Gostin
Visiting Fellow
Oxford University
Centre for Criminological Research
Oxford
1 August 1985

currently Senior Fellow in Health Law
Harvard University
School of Public Health
Boston, Massachusetts

CHAPTER ONE

Sentencing the mentally disordered offender: a threshold problem

This report is primarily concerned with where potentially dangerous mentally disordered people should be placed. One major and obvious referral agency is the criminal courts. They are where many of the problems begin because courts, often through no fault of their own, place mentally disordered offenders in wholly inappropriate and punitive settings. This chapter addresses three questions. Which offenders should be diverted from the criminal justice system to the mental health system? Why have the courts persistently been forced to sentence seriously mentally disordered people to prison? And why do not courts use all of the sentencing options open to them?

Prison or hospital? A choice for the courts

When a mentally disordered person appears before a court charged with an offence there is an important policy decision to be made – does the court pass a therapeutic disposition such as a hospital order, or a punitive disposition such as a sentence of imprisonment? Strangely, there are no clear guidelines as to which offenders should be diverted from the criminal justice system to the mental health system, particularly in marginal cases.

Cases where the sentence is fixed by law

There are certain instances where the court currently does not have any discretion in deciding whether a person should be given a punitive or a therapeutic sentence. If a person is convicted of murder the court must pass a sentence of life imprisonment: if a person is found unfit to plead or not guilty by reason of insanity the court must make a hospital order with restrictions without limit of time.

There is little justification for having a sentence fixed by law since it cannot possibly be known in each case whether a particular defendant should go to prison or to hospital. The Butler report (Home Office 1975) recommended discretion in sentencing in cases of murder, or where there is a finding of unfitness to plead or not guilty by reason of insanity. Yet there has been no move to alter the law and no formal response to the Butler committee's proposals. A change in the law to give discretion in sentencing to the judge would remove some of the vexed questions attached to the plea of diminished responsibility and the defence of insanity. At present the defendant must prove he was not responsible for what he did. This is a question which is inherently unanswerable and we have seen psychiatrists appearing for both sides with contradictory conclusions as to the mental state of the defendant (the Peter Sutcliffe case, for example).

Although in the eyes of the public this lowers the reputation of psychiatrists, in fact it is the law which is at fault. The question of 'blameworthiness' or 'criminal responsibility' has very little relevance to the central question – whether the person should be sent to prison or to hospital. Further, psychiatrists have no possible way of knowing whether a person was 'responsible' for what he did or the degree of his responsibility. Most mental disorders do not *cause* crime and may be only one factor in a complex network leading to an offence. If the fixed penalty for murder had been abolished, the judge in the Peter Sutcliffe case would have heard psychiatric evidence about the really important question, that is whether he was seriously mentally ill and in need of treatment. The psychiatric testimony as to whether he was 'responsible' for what he did is always likely to produce division and uncertainty within the psychiatric profession. It is therefore proposed that the judge should have the discretion to pass any sentence within his power in cases where the defendant is convicted of murder; and that he should be able to pass any sentence except one of imprisonment in cases where the defendant is found unfit to plead or not guilty by reason of insanity.

The law should, wherever possible, authorise the admission to hospital of offenders who are clearly mentally disordered and who require treatment and care. But questions arise in relation to borderline cases where the person is suffering from a minor form of mental disorder and there is uncertainty as to whether he is treatable.

The treatability criterion

Mental disorder is itself not sufficient justification for admission to hospital. There must also be reasonable certainty that the individual will not simply receive custodial care in hospital but active treatment and rehabilitation. It is important for the mental health services that hospitals are not used for preventive or benign confinement, nor that scarce medical resources are allocated to people who cannot benefit from treatment (Stone 1975). More importantly, it is not in the interest of the offender to be admitted to hospital if he cannot be treated, particularly if his confinement is to be indefinite. Should the offender be unable to receive substantial benefit from the treatment, and thus meet clinical and social criteria of improvement, he may be confined for much longer than the period of imprisonment he would expect to receive if he were to be 'punished' instead of 'treated'. The uncertainty as to the length of confinement, and the difficulty in knowing precisely what change in behaviour is necessary before he can be released may result in a deep sense of unfairness and, ultimately, be counter-therapeutic.

The principle put forward here is that hospital admission should be based upon severe mental disorder for which there is a good prospect of benefit from treatment. This would maximise the therapeutic nature of hospitals and help to prevent society from using psychiatry as a form of benign or preventive confinement – that is, detention which is based, not on what a person has done, but what he *might* do in future. The law must ensure that, if the rationale for confinement is therapeutic, treatment must be available which can alleviate the person's mental distress and help him return to the community.

It is, of course, important to seek to provide care for people suffering from mental disorder, even if there is not a good prospect of benefit from conventional psychiatric treatment. However, in some cases it is preferable that care be provided, wherever possible, within the prison system, where the offender can be assured that his length of detention will be based upon ordinary principles of criminal justice.

The new 'treatability' test in section 37(2) of the Mental Health Act 1983 goes some way towards meeting these principles except that there is no 'treatability' criterion for the major forms of mental disorder (that is, mental illness and severe mental impairment), and a restricted patient can continue to be detailed even if he is not treatable (section 73). For example a patient is now being detained at Park Lane Hospital even though his entire therapeutic team considers him to be sane; clearly he is receiving no psychiatric treatment and his detention in hospital is inappropriate and unfair. Yet, a tribunal was able to order his continued detention in hospital because the Mental Health Act does not require his condition to be susceptible to treatment.

15

The 'treatability' criterion is set out in section 37(2) of the Mental Health Act 1983, and relates only to offenders classified as suffering from psychopathic disorder or mental impairment. In these cases treatment must be 'likely to alleviate or prevent a deterioration of his condition'. Some have argued that since 'medical treatment' is defined in section 145(1) as including nursing and care, habitation and rehabilitation under medical supervision, anyone who might, for example, benefit from nursing would be treatable. However the treatability test should be construed much more rigorously than this. It should have to be clearly shown that the treatment will have some effect on deviant behaviour so that there is a good prospect of alleviation or prevention of deterioration of the mental disorder.

Patient choice

There is an issue which does not have a place in current legislation, but which is worthy of careful consideration. That is the choice of the offender as to whether *he* would consent to a hospital order being made. If there is uncertainty about whether psychiatric treatment would alleviate the offender's condition, it should be permissible for the court to make a hospital order only in respect of those who have expressed a preference for admission to hospital rather than prison. There can be little benefit to a patient if he is clearly not prepared to cooperate with treatment (Gunn 1979). The two categories of mental disorder where there are the most persistent doubts about 'treatability' and 'patient choice' are psychopathic disorder and mental impairment.

Psychopathic disorder

One of the great dilemmas in forensic psychiatry is whether it is proper to use compulsory mental health powers over certain repetitive offenders who may be characterised as suffering from psychopathic disorder or other personality disorder. In order to justify the use of such powers it must be shown that psychopathy is a meaningful clinical entity which serves as a valid description of some underlying physiological or psychological disorder; that the disorder can be diagnosed with at least some reliability and objectivity; and that those suffering from the disorder can benefit from psychiatric treatment. The evidence to support each of these assumptions is highly equivocal.

It is clear from the literature that the concept of psychopathy is

16

thought of in psychiatry as being meaningful. There is considerable agreement as to the characteristics of the label, including not being able to profit from experience, lack of control over impulses, recurrent anti-social behaviour and inability to experience guilt (Cleckley 1964; Albert and others 1959; Gray and Hutchison 1964). There are, however, considerable difficulties associated with the use of listed signs or symptoms in determining whether psychopathy is a useful concept. The signs identified by psychiatrists have been numerous and highly diverse. It has been observed that psychopathy is a label which may be attached to a person for a variety of reasons, and that subsequently a large number of signs may be drawn upon to substantiate the application of the label (Davies and Feldman 1981). Although there are a number of signs used to justify the label, there is no agreement on which, if any, are the crucial ones.

In referring to the concept of psychopathic disorder, it must be observed that there has never been any evidence that psychiatrists can objectively identify the characteristics of psychopathic disorder in offenders and make a reliable diagnosis: there does not appear to be any clear distinction between the behaviour of ordinary offenders and those diagnosed as psychopaths. The features of psychopathy listed in the journals appear highly subjective and would require fine judgments to be made. What are the objective indicators, for example, of the signs 'not profiting from experience', 'emotionally immature' or 'lack of moral sense'? More importantly, there does not appear to be any homogeneity in the features of psychopathy which range from recurrent anti-social behaviour (the gravity of the behaviour not being specified) to irresponsible sexual behaviour, excessive alcohol consumption, greater than average intelligence, occupational instability and homosexuality.

There could be other indicators of a valid clinical entity, such as the existence of a demonstrable aetiology or that some objective improvement could be measured from psychiatric intervention. Yet, there is also a multiplicity of opinions as to the cause of, and treatment for, psychopathy. Psychopathic disorder is a concept which appears to be understood, if at all, only by reference to the particular sense in which it is being employed by the individual practitioner. Treatment theories for psychopathic disorder have been as diverse as physical or drug treatment (usually reporting short-term success and lacking both control and long-term follow-up); open or therapeutic communities; and the use of strict supervision and control. There have been no properly controlled studies which have shown any one method of treatment to be clearly more effective than another. It appears that there are no agreed criteria for assessing the 'treatability' of psychopaths and no agreed combination or sequence of therapeutic procedures (see Home Office 1975).

The Mental Health Act 1983 is one of the few major mental health statutes which continues to employ the term 'psychopathic disorder'; the classification is not used in the legislation of Scotland or Northern Ireland. Psychopathic disorder as such is not part of the World Health Organization's International Classification of Diseases, although it is referred to in definitions of personality disorders. The WHO has referred to the compulsory admission of psychopathic patients as one of 'the most serious problems in the British mental health system' (Curran and Harding 1978).

The consultative document (DHSS 1976) and White Paper (DHSS 1978) on the Mental Health Act 1959 said that the National Health Service could not at present offer effective treatment for people classified as psychopathic. However, the Government did not recommend the removal of the classification from the Act because one could not rule out the possibility of a future advance in treatment for this disorder. This reasoning is flawed, for it is difficult to justify the use of compulsory powers today by anticipating some possible benefit in the future. The Mental Health Act 1983 did not alter the definition of psychopathic disorder.

Even if it were possible to conclude from the evidence that psychopathic disorder is a single and recognisable clinical entity, it would still be difficult to maintain the classification for legally relevant purposes. If the rationale for detention was psychopathic disorder alone it would be reasonable to insist that it was necessary to show that the offender would benefit from treatment; there would be no convincing rationale for admission to hospital instead of prison, unless the offender himself expressly chose a therapeutic alternative (see above).

In sum, psychopathic disorder appears to be a most elusive concept: psychiatrists disagree on the meaning of the term and over its diagnosis in particular cases. Some would limit it to a narrow group of dangerously anti-social individuals, while others extend it to cover inadequates of various descriptions, including those with social, sexual, drug or alcoholic deviances (Gibbens 1961). The concept is intractable, and the behaviour of those so classified overlaps with ordinary offenders; there is no demonstrably effective therapy; and the label has proved stigmatic, harmful and indelible. Psychopathic disorder is defined in the Mental Health Act 1983 (Section 1(2)) as a persistent disability of mind which results in abnormally aggressive or seriously irresponsible conduct. (Would serious irresponsibility include, for example, excessive gambling or unwise spending?) It appears that the most important aspect of the term is not the presence of a specific mental condition but its expression in some form of anti-social behaviour. This suggests a rather tautological definition in that it infers a disease from anti-social behaviour, while purporting to explain the behaviour by a disease. The concept of 'personality disorder' may in future present some interesting possible factors in influencing a person's behaviour and, to this end, further research would be of some intrinsic value. The concept does not, however, aid us in making sensible choices about who should be confined, where, and for how long. A person's future liberty should be based upon his past behaviour. This method of determining the length of confinement is fair because it holds a person accountable for his own acts. It puts him in a position similar to others in society who are judged, not because of what they are (or rather how they are perceived by 'experts'), but because of what they have done. Agency, volition and social determination are all important aspects of human behaviour, which is not mechanistic and cannot be predicted purely on a biochemical, clinical or scientific basis.

The guiding principle put forward here is that if the classification of psychopathy is to have any relevance in law at all, it should be based upon the clear preference of the offender for hospital as opposed to prison. There must still be some prospect of benefit from treatment and the offender should receive a finite sentence based upon the gravity of the offence. This puts into effect the overriding principle in forensic psychiatry – which is the level of responsibility that the offender is capable of exercising. The concept of choice in respect of sentencing would say to the offender 'you have offended against the criminal law, you are not entirely responsible for your actions, but you are responsible enough to be given a choice; either you accept ordinary punishment for this offence or you accept a course of medical treatment' (Gunn 1979).

Mental handicap

Mental handicap is in many respects quite different from psychopathic disorder, and certainly more complex. As with psychopathic disorder, it is difficult to accept that direct benefit from treatment should not be an important criterion for a hospital order to be made in respect of a mentally handicapped person. However, it is increasingly recognised that mental handicap is not essentially a medical condition which can benefit from conventional psychiatric treatment in hospital (Gostin 1978, 1979). If the *condition* of being handicapped were to be the exclusive basis for confinement in hospital there could be no reasonably defined period after which hospital confinement would be expected to cease since it is unlikely that the condition itself would be alleviated. The needs of mentally handicapped people are more likely to be social and educational than psychiatric. Accordingly, if exoneration from punishment were to be on the basis of the person's best interests, the alternative to prison would more likely be a guardianship or probation order. This would allow supervised care in the community.

The Mental Health Act 1983 replaces the definition and terminology of mental subnormality with 'mental impairment'. *Mental impairment* is defined as 'a state of arrested or incomplete development of mind which includes significant impairment of intelligence and social functioning and is associated with aggressive or seriously irresponsible conduct'. The term *severe mental impairment* is defined in the same way, except that it encompasses 'severe' (as opposed to 'significant') impairment of intelligence and social functioning (section 1(2)). The legal difference between 'severe' and 'significant' is by no means clear, reflecting only a subtle difference in emphasis.

The terms 'mental impairment' and 'severe mental impairment' are an amalgamation of the old definition of subnormality and psychopathic disorder. Accordingly no mentally handicapped person whose condition is not associated with aggressive or seriously irresponsible conduct can be subject to a hospital or guardianship order.

Arguably the requirement to show a connection with 'abnormally aggressive or seriously irresponsible conduct' would not affect a court's sentencing powers, because in any case where the person has committed an offence there is aggressive or irresponsible behaviour. However, the definition suggests some current association with such behaviour. In many cases the mentally disordered person commits an offence from quite sound motives, such as hunger, jealousy, anger or greed. It may be difficult to demonstrate that there is any particular relationship between the person's mental condition and a pattern of behaviour. Further, it should be asked whether an isolated offence, without additional medical or social evidence, gives grounds for showing a connection with a pattern of aggressive or irresponsible behaviour. Courts should require doctors who give evidence to address themselves fully to the question of whether the offender meets the criterion for mental impairment under the Act.

The question arises whether a mentally handicapped person convicted of an offence should be admitted to hospital or to prison. (This assumes that a guardianship order or other non-custodial disposition is inappropriate; see below.) There are serious problems connected with sentencing a mentally handicapped person to a term of imprisonment. Mentally handicapped people, particularly if they function in the lower ranges of intelligence and social competence, would have difficulty in coping with a prison environment. The discipline and rigidity often make it an unacceptable alternative for reasons of compassion. It could be reasonably argued that admission to a local mental handicap hospital would be more humane from the patient's perspective than a sentence of imprisonment. This dilemma needs to be carefully considered in each case. Certainly, a mentally handicapped person's choice of a hospital order instead of imprisonment should not prejudice his length of confinement and right to a periodic review of the need for his detention.

The issue of offender-preference is also more complex in the case of mental handicap. It is wrong to suggest that all mentally handicapped people cannot make a reasonable choice between prison and hospital; many patients have very strong views which should be respected. There will be cases of severely mentally handicapped people where the ability to choose will be restricted and this problem must be recognised. The principle, however, still stands that a person's choice, whenever possible, should be respected.

Clearly a severely mentally impaired person will not have the competence to choose between prison and hospital, and residing in prison would be cruel and inappropriate. For example, in *Cornwell's* case a severely mentally handicapped woman (aged 18 with a mental age of nine) was forcibly tattooed while in prison. It is proposed, therefore, that severely mentally impaired people should *never* be sentenced to a term of imprisonment; and that mentally impaired people should have the choice whether or not to consent to a hospital order.

'Abnormally aggressive or seriously irresponsible conduct'

The new definition of mental impairment was intended to prevent the long-term detention of mentally handicapped people unless they were 'abnormally aggressive' or 'seriously irresponsible'. There is reason to be extremely critical of these words used in the Act. It leaves quite unclear the evidence which is needed to fulfil these criteria. Is conduct in the distant past acceptable or need there be *current* behaviour? Can a single incident suffice or should it be a pattern of behaviour? Moreover, the concepts of 'aggression' and 'irresponsibility' are hardly grave enough to justify potentially long-term deprivation of liberty. 'Aggression' can include situational anger or argumentative behaviour which often is understandable and is never a good justification for removal of a person's liberty. 'Irresponsibility' is a subjective term and is in many ways judgmental. It could include self-neglect or behaviour which is unconventional or annoying.

It is proposed that only patients who have exhibited recent overt behaviour which is a serious danger to themselves or others should be classified as mentally impaired and liable to longer-term detention in hospital.

Sentencing a mentally disordered person to imprisonment

Often there is no doubt that a person is mentally disordered and in need of hospital treatment, but the court has to pass a sentence of imprisonment. This means that an offender who could be seriously mentally ill or mentally handicapped goes into prison where the regime is hard and inflexible and there is very little, if any, opportunity for treatment and care. Such an environment is cruel and will probably result in a deterioration in the person's mental condition; and his presence is disruptive to the running of the prison and unfair to prison officers and other prisoners.

Why is it that a court which is fully satisfied on the basis of two medical opinions that the offender is mentally disordered and in need of hospital care, often has no power to make a hospital order?

Section 37(4) of the Mental Health Act 1983 states that a hospital order 'shall not be made under this section unless the court is satisfied on the written or oral evidence of the registered medical practitioner who would be in charge of his treatment or of some other person representing the managers of the hospital that arrangements have been made for his admission to that hospital . . . '. This puts the judge in an unfamiliar position as regards his sentencing powers. He cannot make a hospital order unless the hospital managers (that is, the district health authority or, in the case of the special hospitals, the DHSS) agree to take the offender. In practice the decision to make a bed available is taken by a consultant. There have been many cases in which doctors or the DHSS have refused to make a bed available for the offender; hence the judge, although he heard the requisite medical evidence, could not make a hospital order. The court's frustration with this situation was succinctly stated by Mr Justice Mais in the case of *Brazil*: 'I find it hard to understand how it is that an order of this court is apparently incapable of being carried out' (see also *R v Gordon*).

The courts have made every attempt to impose their judgments upon hospital authorities but often to no avail. In the cases of *Brazil* and *Arant* the judge sternly admonished the appropriate officials; in *Nicholl's* case, Lord Justice Edmund Davies became 'very disturbed about this situation' and adjourned the case for the third time in order for the 'Secretary of State to give further consideration to the matter'. In perhaps the strongest statement of judicial consternation, Lord Justice Lawton in *R v Officer* said:

> From time to time in the past decade judges had been put in the position of having to sentence to prison for life, persons who clearly ought to have gone to a mental hospital. Judges took the judicial oath of office to do justice by all men. When they had in the past to send persons to prison because no beds were available in a secure hospital, their judicial consciences were strained almost to breaking point. It is hoped that in such cases, that kind of problem will never arise again.'

In *Marsden's* case the court found there was no vacancy in any hospital within the region of the Quarter Sessions. Accordingly, it concluded that an order may be made for admission to a hospital in any part of the country where a vacancy exists.

The most forceful attempt by a court to compel hospitals to admit mentally disordered offenders came in *R v Harding*. Lord Justice

Lawton said that 'anyone who obstructed the execution of [a hospital] order or procured others to obstruction might be guilty of contempt of court.' In *Harding's* case there was general agreement that he should be admitted to a regional secure unit. However, because of industrial action by nurses he was unable to be admitted. The Court of Appeal suggested that such unlawful obstruction was a contempt of court. Surely the Court of Appeal was wrong, for making a bed available in a suitable hospital is *a condition precedent* to making a hospital order; by section 37(4) no order can be made until a bed is available. Thus a failure to make a bed available could not obstruct the execution of the order. It is conceivable, however, that once the managers arrange for admission and a hospital order has been duly made, an unlawful obstruction of that order could be contempt.

New solutions in the Mental Health Act

During the parliamentary debates preceding the Mental Health (Amendment) Act 1982 there was considerable discussion of the problems facing courts in making hospital orders. Indeed, the Special Standing Committee on the Mental Health (Amendment) Bill tied in a vote to give the courts power to compel hospitals to admit mentally disordered offenders. At report stage in the House of Commons it was agreed to provide the courts with assistance to overcome these difficulties while continuing to give ultimate discretion to the managers to refuse admission to hospitals. Thus, section 39 of the Mental Health Act 1983 allows a court which is minded to make a hospital order, or an interim hospital order, to request the regional health authority (or, in Wales, the Secretary of State for Wales) to furnish information about hospitals where arrangements could be made for admission of the offender. The RHA cannot avoid responsibility, because the court is empowered to request information from *any* appropriate RHA and the information to be given could relate to *any* region.

The Mental Health Act 1983 (sections 35, 36, 38) also introduced remands to hospital for treatment or for report, and interim hospital orders. These new provisions provide an opportunity for a person brought before a court to be examined or treated in hospital before the court makes its final decision. This should act as an encouragement to hospitals to take mentally disordered offenders because, initially, it can be for a trial period. These provisions had resource implications and were not implemented with the rest of the Act (section 149), but they were brought into force in October 1984.

The reasons why hospital authorities and the DHSS have, on occasion, resisted a court's request to make a bed available in a hospital are discussed below. In some instances they involve genuine differences of clinical opinion; in others, administrative difficulties.

No bed available in a special hospital

In several cases, the Court of Appeal has said that, before making a hospital order with restrictions, a crown court should ascertain which hospital will receive the offender and ensure that the hospital has facilities for keeping him in safe custody (for example, *R v Morris*; *R v Higginbotham*; *R v Cox*). Here clinical disputes can develop: the doctor giving evidence before the court may consider that the offender requires a high security hospital, while the DHSS and the special hospital consultants disagree and refuse to make a bed available. Admission to a maximum security institution has enormous consequences for the liberty of the subject. The special hospitals are, therefore, correct in seeking to ensure that only the most dangerous offenders are admitted. The difficulty is that if no secure accommodation is made available, the court may pass a sentence of imprisonment, even though a local hospital is prepared to accept the offender. This occurred in *Farrell's* case where the doctor giving evidence before the court described him as a dangerous psychopath and recommended admission to a special hospital. The DHSS refused to make a bed available, saying that 'treatment could be given in a less secure hospital'. In *Ryan's* case, an 18 year old boy was convicted of causing criminal damage by fire. No local hospital would have him because of the fire risk. The DHSS also refused a bed in a special hospital, but without examining the offender. The Chester crown court said: 'It is crystal clear from the medical reports that he is severely mentally ill. He may die and there is no suggestion of his being committed to prison. . . . The situation is scandalous.'

In the case of *Ian Officer* the Court of Appeal said: ' . . . the judge was placed in a position in which no judge should ever be placed by the Department. He had before him reports of two consultant psychiatrists of outstanding experience. Both were agreed that the appellant should be detained in a secure hospital and there could not have been a clearer case for a patient to go to a secure hospital but, because no doctor from Broadmoor had examined him and there was no intimation by the Department that a bed was available, Mr Justice Willis had no alternative but to send the appellant to life imprisonment.'

No bed available in a local hospital

One of the most marked changes in the mental health services since the Percy commission (Royal Commission 1957) sat from 1954–1957 is that hospitals have developed 'open-door' policies. (See further below.) This has resulted in local hospitals being unwilling to admit mentally disordered offenders who may be difficult or dangerous.

There have been numerous examples over the years of the courts having great difficulty in finding a bed in a local NHS hospital for mentally disordered offenders. In *Suchodolski's* case the Liverpool crown court reported that four doctors had said he should be treated under non-secure conditions. Yet no local hospital was prepared to take him because they considered their security inadequate. In the case of *Twigger*, the Central Criminal Court was forced to sentence the defendant to life imprisonment after four mental hospitals had refused to accept him. Finally, in *Smith's* case the Shrewsbury crown court was forced to sentence her to nine months' imprisonment for stealing 36 pence after psychiatrists in local hospitals had refused to take her because of the effect they thought she would have on other patients in an open ward.

Anthony Ledger had spent two and a half years in and out of prisons and mental hospitals. His offences were trivial, including stealing a toy, stealing a bag of coal, and taking a free ride on the railway. He was considered mentally ill but no hospital would accept him because he might be too disruptive for an open-door institution. One doctor said to the court: 'The realities are that the National Health Service mental hospitals will not now accept responsibility for such cases as Mr Ledger. Having abandoned all forms of security control they can now claim that they have no facilities for the treatment of patients with aspects of dangerousness. . . . The prison medical service will therefore be compelled to face the task that should more properly be the responsibility of others.' The court felt that it had no choice but to pass a sentence of imprisonment for 18 months.

For ten years now local branches of the Confederation of Health Service Employees (COHSE) have been refusing to accept mentally disordered offenders from the courts and the special hospitals. In

R v Brazil a Bristol crown court judge made an order for the admission of the offender to Glenside Hospital but COHSE members refused to admit him. No one on the nursing staff had seen the doctor's reports on Mr Brazil or saw him personally. The court expressed 'extreme difficulty' in understanding how this action could be taken without first trying to assess his needs.

Immediately after *Brazil's* case the union's National Executive decided:

> That nurses should be able to choose whether they want to work with, or near, abnormal offenders in mental hospitals if they consider safety and security provisions are not adequate ... This decision will continue until the union is satisfied that the level of the treatment facilities do not expose nursing staff to unacceptable degrees of bodily danger.

Remarkably, the decision has still not been reversed. Since the publicity given to the *Brazil* case, and no doubt as a consequence of trade union activities, there have been many cases in which hospital staff refused would-be patients from the courts. The DHSS (1976) in an attempt to reduce the anxieties of hospital staff, issued a circular on the management of violent or potentially violent patients. COHSE instructed its members to ignore the DHSS guidance, and subsequently issued its own guidelines (COHSE 1977).

Ashingdane's case, which was recently decided by the European Court of Human Rights, first arose because of the industrial dispute by COHSE. Mr Ashingdane, a patient at Broadmoor Hospital, was recommended for transfer to Oakwood in Kent by his Broadmoor consultant and a Mental Health Review Tribunal. The recommendation was supported by the Secretary of State for Social Services and the Home Secretary. The consultant at Oakwood Hospital was also prepared to make a bed available. But the transfer was blocked by COHSE members. MIND brought a case on behalf of Mr Ashingdane against the Secretary of State, the area health authority and two named COHSE members. The action against the health authority and the Secretary of State was barred by section 141 of the Mental Health Act 1959 (now section 139 of the 1983 Act), and was the subject of the recent European Court case. The Court of Appeal allowed the action against COHSE to proceed, but the action was settled before it was decided on the merits. Arguably the Secretary of State has a statutory duty to provide hospital accommodation suited to a person's needs, and a future case could establish this point now that section 139 excludes the Secretary of State from protection against litigation. Nurses in mental illness and mental handicap hospitals take primary responsibility for the day-to-day care of patients. They remain with patients in a sheltered environment for long periods, sometimes without the full support and understanding of the managers and medical staff. They have an absolute right to be fully consulted before any decisions are taken to admit potentially difficult or dangerous patients; and they have a right to expect to receive full support.

On the other hand, it should be pointed out that nursing is a profession, and part of the essence of a profession is that the defence of its status and interests cannot properly be separated from the maintenance of its standards of performance. In seeking to obtain more support and a fair share of resources, nurses should not deprive patients of their basic right to treatment in the least restrictive setting possible. The staff in a local hospital must keep in mind that if they refuse to take a patient from the court he may quite inappropriately be sent to prison or a special hospital. It is a failure of the overall provision of the National Health Service when a patient who does not need high security and for whom no bed is available locally is placed in a special hospital (with all the stigma and deprivation of liberty that is entailed) or a prison.

In Chapter 4 it is recommended that there should be more and better trained staff in local hospitals, and that they should have the facilities to help deal with potentially dangerous patients.

Consultants at some hospitals have also been reluctant to accept offenders from the courts. Their refusal sometimes arises from a genuine difference of clinical opinion in evidence to the court. Others refuse for less particular reasons. For example, a psychiatrist may feel that the presence of a potentially dangerous patient could cause concern in the local community. It should be part of his job to reduce such concern and, of course, his primary responsibility must be to his patients. A local hospital should not close its doors to people in need because there is a small chance that they may cause a disturbance. If a court of law is prepared on the basis of medical and other evidence to send the offender to a non-secure hospital, that hospital should be prepared to take the risk. If, after admitting the offender, the local hospital finds it cannot cope, there should be a sympathetic review of the patient's suitability for a special hospital or secure unit.

Proposals for reform

One of the most difficult problems in the NHS is to determine how to break down the formidable barriers which have arisen in trying to obtain care for mentally disordered offenders in relatively open conditions. The main barrier is an attitudinal one which cannot be altered with a change in law or policy. The following suggestions are, however, intended to help reduce the impediments to access to care.

1 *Role of the hospital managers*
There can be no doubt that under the Mental Health Act 1983 the hospital manager has the sole responsibility for making a bed available. Clearly managers will want to consult with medical, nursing and other staff, but they should take the final decision. Unfortunately this does not occur at present, and managers play only the most nominal part in making decisions; in practice, they have delegated their authority to consultants.

This is wrong as a matter of law and policy, for it is intended that managers should take decisions about how resources will be allocated and whether care will be offered equally to every category of patient in need of mental hospital services. The National Health Service Act 1977 requires the Secretary of State for Social Services to provide services 'to such an extent as he considers necessary to meet *all reasonable requirements.*' This basic duty is delegated to regional health authorities and then to district health authorities. Health authorities should actively ensure that all reasonable requirements are met and that a fair share of resources is devoted to secure provision.

2 *Compelling hospitals to admit patients from the courts*
During the parliamentary debates on the Mental Health (Amendment) Act 1982, MIND and other groups supported an amendment that hospital managers should, where appropriate, be compelled by the courts to admit mentally disordered offenders. The vote on the amendment was tied in committee and eventually lost. The argument against such a provision is that doctors and nurses should not be forced to admit patients whom they think they cannot help; further, it would not be in the patients' interests to be

29

cared for by unwilling staff. There is some truth in the argument; and it must be recalled that sometimes it is the court which wishes to place offenders inappropriately in special hospitals when there is no real need for secure treatment. However, the logic is flawed because often the hospital has no specific reason for refusing to admit the patient and, sometimes, staff have not even examined the patient. Nurses must care for patients whom the doctor agrees to take; this is also true of prison officers. There may still be a case for giving courts the power to order the admission of a patient. Those who are to be responsible for the care of the patient would give evidence to the court and it is to be assumed that the court would listen very carefully to their advice. This proposal was endorsed by the Parliamentary All-Party Penal Affairs Group (1980). If it is not acceptable there are other alternative avenues to explore (see below).

3 *Statutory duty to provide services*
It was explained above that health authorities have a basic duty to provide services to meet 'all reasonable requirements'. If it is considered that compelling an authority in an individual case is wrong in principle, it should still be possible to give the authority a more precise statutory duty to provide services. The National Health Service Act already lists the kinds of services which must be provided. It would be helpful to refer specifically to hospital services for mentally disordered offenders or to seek some other way to strengthen the statutory duty and make it more specific and comprehensible to health authorities.

4 *Formulation of standards and a duty to examine*
The DHSS should issue a circular to all district health authorities (DHAs) instructing them in their duties under the Mental Health Act and National Health Service Act and saying that they will be held accountable for failure to carry out their duties properly under the acts. The DHAs would be expected to formulate reasonable standards for the admission of patients by referring to maximum numbers, minimum conditions of care and treatment, and the specific psychiatric condition of the prospective patient (irrespective of his legal status under the Mental Health Act).

Sentencing policy in dealing with offenders suffering from mental disorder*

Courts have a range of 'therapeutic' disposals available to them but there is very little guidance as to which sentence to choose in a particular case. Among the dispositions now available are hospital orders with or without restrictions on discharge, guardianship orders, and probation orders with a condition of psychiatric treatment.

The task of deciding which disposition is preferable should be based upon the following general principle: the law should facilitate treatment where it is possible and available; the person should receive treatment in the least restrictive setting necessary for the safety of the public; and the person should not be deprived of liberty for a longer period than is justified by the nature and gravity of the offence.

Where the offender is suffering from a form of mental disorder which is treatable, and where the facilities for treatment are available, the court should avoid passing a sentence of imprisonment. In some cases, an absolute or conditional discharge will be sufficient if the court is satisfied that the offender will undertake or continue a course of treatment. A fine or an ordinary probation order may be appropriate in other cases, particularly if the mental disorder is not significantly disabling. (In *Skelton* a recorder took the unusual course of deferring sentence for six months on the defendant's undertaking to reside in a mental hospital. This may have been an unwise use of the power to defer sentence since a short psychiatric probation order would have been preferable, but the Court of Appeal quite wrongly held that the recorder's use of the power to defer was *unlawful*.)

When a court considers that it should pass some 'therapeutic' alternative, the possibilities to be considered are the psychiatric probation order, the hospital order and the guardianship order.

Psychiatric probation order

While the psychiatric probation order may be appropriate in many cases where neither the mental disorder nor the offence is so serious as to call for a hospital order, decisions of the Court of Appeal show that it may also be used in cases which might otherwise warrant a

*This section is taken from Ashworth and Gostin (1984).

substantial custodial sentence (*R v Hayes*). Where the mental disorder is treatable a psychiatric probation order may well provide a greater degree of public protection than a prison sentence. The treatment which only the order can provide may ameliorate the mental disorder and thus, possibly, help to reduce the offending in the long term, as the Court of Appeal recognised in *Nicholls*. Although Lewis (1980) suggested that liaison between the supervising probation officer and the psychiatrist has sometimes been poor, a court may exercise some control by asking each to submit a report on the offender – say every six months. Thus a psychiatric probation order should be seen as a flexible order which will often be appropriate when the conduct of the offender and the cooperation of a probation officer and a psychiatrist can be relied upon. As the least intrusive of the three orders upon the offender's liberty, it should be considered first. It is intended for cases where the person's mental condition does not warrant detention in pursuance of a hospital order. Neither a hospital order nor a guardianship order should be chosen unless it is the 'most suitable' means of dealing with the offender.

Guardianship order

If a psychiatric probation order will not provide the care, treatment and support required, the court should consider a guardianship order. A guardianship order may also be appropriate in cases where the offender refuses to consent to a probation order and some degree of supervision is necessary to ensure that he receives treatment, care, habilitation or training in the community. It would be preferable to a hospital order where there is no immediate risk to the public and it is desirable that therapeutic objectives are met in a less restrictive community setting.

Guardianship orders are seldom used. In any year only a handful are made (Home Office 1983). This is unfortunate as they provide a useful alternative to detention in hospital. They can be particularly helpful in meeting the needs of mentally impaired offenders who could benefit from occupation, training and education in the community. Guardianship orders are often the most preferable sentences for mentally handicapped people. They are not suffering from a medical illness which requires hospital treatment and could suffer badly in a prison, and not get the treatment they need. In most cases, a guardianship order could provide a less restrictive setting in which care and habilitation could take place.

Hospital orders

Hospital orders should be reserved for cases in which they are the 'most suitable' measure. They require the court to consider and dismiss each alternative means of dealing with the offender, and to take account of the effects which come from making the order. Although a hospital order is 'therapeutic' in intention, it involves a deprivation of liberty, particularly when there is a restriction order attached. Accordingly, a hospital order should never be used unless the offence is serious enough to warrant a custodial order. Also, it should not be used unless the offender is suffering from a major form of mental disorder which is treatable. The element of patient choice should also be a relevant consideration, particularly in the case of patients suffering from minor forms of mental disorder, such as psychopathic disorder. Restriction orders should accompany a hospital order only in cases where it is absolutely necessary to protect the public from serious harm. In *A Human Condition* (Gostin 1977) MIND recommended that the length of detention under a restriction order should not be disproportionate to the gravity of the offence and the antecedents of the offender. As a general proposition this remains as valid today.

Sentence of imprisonment

Sometimes courts pass a sentence of imprisonment for quite inappropriate reasons. Perhaps the most frequent is for an offence which, if the offender were not mentally disordered, would result in the loss of liberty for one, two or three years. Were he to be sent to a local hospital he might abscond and re-offend. The availability of a place in a regional secure unit might help to solve the problem but in many cases a place in a secure unit or a special hospital is inappropriate or unavailable.

If a place in a local hospital is available and the mentally disordered offender's condition is treatable, should the court make a hospital order in the knowledge that it cannot guarantee security, or should it impose a sentence of imprisonment simply to ensure that the public is protected for a given period? Since a hospital place is available, the proper course is surely to make a hospital order. The amount of public protection provided by a prison sentence of, say, two years, can be over-estimated. 'Public protection' means avoiding the risk that a member of the public will fall victim to a certain kind of offence within a given period. Removing one offender from circulation for 16 months (two years less remission) is likely to have an infinitesimal effect on that risk in the short term. Were the offender placed in an environment where he will receive treatment (in a hospital, not a prison) there is at least the possibility of a longer-term amelioration of the mental condition and, consequently, of the offender's behaviour. If sent to prison, he will be released without treatment, possibly in worse condition than before. This is reflected in the statement by J McCullough in *Gordon*: imprisonment '. . . might not just be wrong in the sense that it did not provide the best solution for her, but might positively cause harm, because imprisonment might lead to her deterioration.'

Frequently, courts feel that they have no alternative but to impose a sentence of imprisonment or youth custody on a mentally disordered offender. Since it is widely agreed that prison is an inappropriate and sometimes damaging environment for many persons suffering from mental disorder, the justifications for these sentences must be scrutinised with great care. The most difficult cases are those in which the offender's disorder is said to be treatable, but there is no hospital place available. The courts have made vehement protests about this predicament (see above) and occasionally a hospital place has been found when the case has come before the Court of Appeal.

Granted that these cases arise, how is the court to approach sentence? If the sentencer looks to the Court of Appeal's decisions for guidance, he will find a hopelessly confused jumble of rulings. On the one hand there is the principle that the courts should not use the prisons in order to 'make up for the deficiency in the medical and social services,' trenchantly stated in *Clarke*, followed in *Tolley* and in *Slater* and re-asserted by the court in *Fisher*: '. . . the sentences to be imposed . . . must of course be commensurate with the offence in question.' Thus, if the mentally disordered person has spent many years in and out of institutions, has committed a trivial offence, and there is no bed available in the National Health Service, he should not be given a prison sentence. Rather, he should be given a non-custodial sentence such as a fine or conditional discharge, just as would have happened had he not been mentally disordered.

On the other hand, there is the line of cases in which the Court of Appeal has accepted that the prison sentence is 'too long for the offence itself' but has nonetheless upheld it on grounds of public protection: *Arrowsmith*, *Scanlon*, *Walsh* and most brazenly in *Gouws*.

Here, the courts appear to be saying that if the offender is mentally disordered and there is a prediction of future dangerous behaviour then the courts can impose a sentence of imprisonment longer than that justified by the offence itself or the antecedents of the offender. The Court of Appeal has not taken the trouble to consider these rulings together and to explain, to sentencers and others, the reasons for taking different approaches and the factors which distinguish the cases. Clearly, it is the first principle which is to be preferred. Proportionality between the offence and the length of imprisonment ought to be the guiding consideration. As a Home Office study concluded: 'predictions of future behaviour are rightly recognised as too fallible to enter into sentencing decisions' (Brody and Tarling 1980). There is insufficient justification for extending the length of detention – for example, by the imposition of a prison sentence longer than would otherwise be given for the offence or by the inappropriate use of a restriction order. Medical evidence suggesting that the offender is mentally disordered and could benefit from treatment should only be an indication for the court to ensure that he is placed in a setting where he will receive care and treatment. The entire range of therapeutic dispositions should be considered and the least restrictive and most therapeutic care setting should be chosen which is compatible with the patient's need for treatment and society's right to be protected.

Summary of recommendations: Sentencing the mentally disordered offender

Sentences fixed by law

1 *The court should have the discretion to pass any sentence within its powers in cases where the defendant is convicted of murder; and the court should have the power to pass any sentence except one of imprisonment in cases where the defendant is found unfit to plead or not guilty by reason of insanity.*

'Treatability' and patient choice

2 *As a general principle, hospital admission should be based upon a severe form of mental disorder for which there is a good prospect of benefit from treatment:*
   a) *patients should not be admitted to hospital unless treatment is likely to ameliorate or prevent a deterioration in their condition;*

b) *patients suffering from minor forms of mental disorder (that is, psychopathic disorder or mental impairment) where there is no reasonable expectation that their condition is 'treatable' should have the right to refuse admission to hospital.*

Psychopathic disorder

3 *Since 'psychopathic disorder' is an elusive concept which different psychiatrists view in different ways and since there is rarely a good prospect of benefit from treatment, offenders should usually be sentenced to imprisonment (if appropriate) rather than be given a hospital order. A hospital order should be used only where the offender chooses this alternative and where doctors feel there may be some reasonable possibility of constructive treatment.*

Mental impairment

4 *If a mentally handicapped person is to be compulsorily admitted or detained in hospital it must be clearly shown that his condition is currently associated with a pattern of dangerous behaviour:*
   a) *courts should require doctors to address themselves fully to the question of whether the offender meets the criterion for 'mental impairment' under the Act;*
   b) *severely mentally impaired people should never be sentenced to a term of imprisonment; and mentally impaired people should have the choice whether to consent to a hospital order.*

5 *The definition of 'mental impairment' should be amended so that 'dangerousness to self or others as shown by recent overt behaviour' should replace 'abnormally aggressive or seriously irresponsible conduct'.*

Nurses' reluctance to admit mentally disordered offenders

6 *Every effort should be made to provide nurses in local hospitals with staffing and other resources, training and guidance to help them care for mentally disordered offenders (see Chapter 4):*
   a) *nurses and managers should be encouraged to seek ways to defend their wages and conditions of service without resort to action which harms patients;*
   b) *the industrial action by COHSE should be the subject of renewed negotiation which adheres to the above principles.*

Admission of mentally disordered offenders to hospital

7 *The hospital managers should take the decision as to admission of*

mentally disordered offenders to hospital in consultation with their multi-disciplinary team.

8 *Further consideration should be given to empowering the courts to compel hospitals to admit patients under a hospital order.*

9 *The Secretary of State should have a clearer statutory duty (delegatable to health authorities) to provide hospital and other services for mentally disordered offenders.*

10 *The DHSS should issue a circular to all district health authorities instructing them as to their statutory duties to provide services, and setting out minimum standards of care and treatment for mentally disordered offenders.*

Sentencing and detention

11 *There should be three general principles for sentencing and detaining mentally disordered offenders:*
   a) *the law should facilitate treatment where it is possible and available;*
   b) *the person should receive treatment in the least restrictive setting necessary for the safety of the public;*
   c) *a person should not be deprived of liberty longer than is justified by the nature and gravity of the offence.*

12 *As a* **psychiatric probation order** *is the least intrusive on the person's liberty of the three 'therapeutic' orders, it should be considered first by the courts.*

13 *More use should be made of* **guardianship orders,** *particularly for mentally impaired offenders who could benefit from occupation, training and education in the community.*

14 **Hospital orders** *should be reserved for cases in which a non-custodial order is inappropriate because of the risk to the public. It is only where the risk is probable and serious that a restriction order should be added.*

15 *If a place in a local hospital is available and the offender is clearly mentally disordered and 'treatable', the court should not pass a* **sentence of imprisonment.**

16 *The Court of Appeal should give guidance as to sentencing mentally disordered offenders:*
   a) *it should re-affirm the principle that the sentence must be commensurate with the offence in question;*
   b) *medical evidence alone should not be a basis for a longer period of detention.*

CHAPTER TWO

Mentally disordered people in the prison system

Scope of the problem

The failure of sentencing policy (see Chapter 1) is immediately apparent when one examines the number of people suffering from mental disorder who are currently in prison. Unlike NHS hospitals, prisons do not have a choice whether or not to accept people sentenced by the court.

Angela is in her thirties and suffers from Huntington's Chorea, whose symptoms include loss of balance, incoherent speech and lack of control over her limbs. She was remanded to Holloway on 1 November 1984 having been charged with arson. She rarely left her cell, spent a great deal of her time alone there and complained of loneliness. Everybody on the staff agreed that she should not be there. Attempts to find appropriate hospital accommodation failed until 1 March when all charges were dropped and the hospital that had originally refused to accept her if she was subjected to a court order under the Mental Health Act, admitted her under a civil section of the Act.

These kinds of cases are dramatic and alarming but they are not isolated incidents. They illustrate the inadequacy in particular of C1 unit which itself has to be set within the context of the inadequacies of Holloway as a whole. Angela was fortunate in finding a hospital bed. Many mentally abnormal offenders are sentenced to imprisonment. A visiting consultant psychiatrist at a local prison wrote: 'Our principal problem remains the difficulty of obtaining beds in mental hospitals for those suffering from psychotic diseases. Matters have become more intricate; at one time the consultant decided who he would admit, but he now has to obtain the consent of his nursing staff ... At present the major problem is schizophrenics in prison where there is little scope for their social rehabilitation'.

A senior medical officer at another local prison wrote: 'The problem of obtaining beds in mental hospitals has remained with us ... the staff in hospitals have remained unwilling to accept or nurse mentally disordered offenders'.

Figures provided by the Prison Medical Service consistently show

38

significant numbers of prisoners awaiting transfer to a NHS hospital. Figures since 30 June 1977 are reproduced in Table 1; they are derived from correspondence between Lord Elton and Lord Avebury (Elton 1983) (see also six-monthly returns by Prison Medical Officers to the Home Office, 1985).

Table 1 Mentally disordered inmates awaiting transfer, 1977–1984

	Sentenced	Unsentenced	Non-criminal	Total
30 June 1977	517	249	3	769
31 December 1977	461	216	5	682
30 June 1978	377	200	4	581
31 December 1978	389	125	5	519
30 June 1979	347	206	4	557
31 December 1979	288	156	2	446
30 June 1980	250	204	3	457
31 December 1980	219	103	2	324
30 June 1981	175	144	1	320
30 September 1981	170	157	0	327
31 March 1982	139	148	0	287
30 September 1982	126	160	0	286
31 March 1983	160	159	0	319
31 March 1984	144	166	0	310

As at 31 March 1984 there were 310 prisoners awaiting transfer, which is slightly more than the figures for 1982; however, the overall trend since 30 June 1977 is markedly down. Most observers regard these as highly conservative figures and somewhat unreliable estimates, since the number actually placed on the transfer list depends upon the prevailing philosophy of imprisonment, the attitudes of mental health professionals and the treatment and care facilities provided in the two systems. The fact is that many prison medical officers have stopped recommending that all of their mentally disordered patients should be transferred to the National Health Service because they have realised that hospital places will not be made available for many of them (see Home Office 1980, para. 161). As it is, many prisoners have been waiting a year or more on the transfer list (see Parliamentary debates 1982a). Further, the great majority on the transfer list in 1984 (235) were suffering from mental illness (a major form of mental disorder) with 24 suffering from mental impairment, 50 from psychopathic disorder and one from severe mental impairment.

Independent studies suggest that between 15 and 20 per cent of all prisoners manifest sufficient psychiatric pathology to warrant attention or intervention (Roth 1980). However, the number manifesting severe psychiatric disturbance is in the order of five per cent (Guze 1976; Gunn and others 1978).

In recent years there have been as many unsentenced prisoners with mental disorder as sentenced prisoners. It is clearly wrong for a mentally disordered person who has not yet been convicted or sentenced to remain in prison without treatment. Recent independent psychiatric evidence tends to show that prison medical officer estimates are indeed on the conservative side. Pamela Taylor and Professor John Gunn carried out a study of prisoners remanded into custody which showed that nine per cent are psychotic, four per cent alcoholic and five per cent drug dependent (Gunn 1985).

Clearly there is a large number of highly vulnerable, emotionally disturbed people in prison in England and Wales. Their characteristics range quite widely, from the overtly psychotic and severely mentally handicapped to those with psychopathic or personality disorder, drug and alcohol dependence and epilepsy. There are many more who simply need asylum but find shelter only in reception centres and prisons. It is apparent that prisons have become institutions which have served as the receptacles of those whom no other agency in society will accept. It is noteworthy that the prison department is the only institution which is not empowered to exercise discretion over its admission policy.

A number of recommendations were made in the previous chapter to seek to prevent the admission of mentally disordered offenders to prison. With the recent introduction of remands to hospital for psychiatric report or treatment, it is to be hoped that it will no longer be necessary to send unsentenced people to prison. However, it is likely for the foreseeable future that a great many people will go to prison who require some kind of psychiatric treatment, care or nursing. The report on the work of the prison department (Home Office 1982) observed that 'apart from the inhumane aspects of committing mentally disordered offenders to prisons and borstals, it is not possible to provide . . . the medical treatment and nursing care their condition requires whilst they are in custody'. Indeed, the

Director-General of the Prison Service in evidence to the Select Parliamentary Committee stated that the Prison Medical Service does not purport to offer comprehensive psychiatric treatment because of the belief that transfers of mentally disordered offenders should be made to the National Health Service (see further Home Office 1979 and Orr 1978).

The Prison Medical Service

England and Wales have the only prison system in the western world to have a large, complex, self-contained Prison Medical Service. (See Gunn 1985) A discussion follows of the Prison Medical Service, together with proposals for it to be amalgamated with the National Health Service.

Treatment

GRENDON UNDERWOOD: PSYCHOTHERAPY

Grendon Underwood in Buckinghamshire was opened in 1962 for selected prisoners thought to need psychiatric observation or treatment. Grendon does not cater for psychotic or mentally handicapped prisoners but for those with personality disorders or neurosis who are of average intelligence or above. Unlike all other prisons, it was governed by a doctor who was a trained psychiatrist. Grendon does not accept inmates direct from the courts but receives them from prisons and borstals at the direction of the Prison Department and upon preliminary investigation by medical officers. The prisoners must consent to going to Grendon.

Grendon operates a therapeutic community and has individual and group psychotherapy. Studies have shown that prisoners there show an increase in social confidence and self-esteem and become easier to manage (Gunn and others 1978). (This is also the position at Barlinnie Prison in Scotland.) However, research conducted by the Home Office produced no significant evidence that reconviction rates are lowered by psychotherapy given at Grendon (Newton 1971; McLean 1975).

Consent

In law any adult prisoner (except those remanded for treatment under section 36 of the Mental Health Act 1983) can refuse treatment under the common law (see Gostin 1985). It does not matter whether he is mentally disordered and the doctor proposes to treat

41

his disorder; he is still entitled to refuse. Lord Elton, Under Secretary of State at the Home Office, accepted this view in Parliament:

> Doctors working in prisons have no statutory authority to administer treatment against the wishes of their patients. It would thus be defensible to treat a prisoner against his wishes only if otherwise his life would be endangered, serious harm to him or to others would be likely or an irreversible deterioration in his condition. Such emergencies are in practice very rare (Parliamentary debates 1982).

In order to give valid consent to treatment under the common law the patient must be informed of the nature and purpose of the treatment; and he must agree voluntarily, without any improper threats or inducements. The question arises whether a prisoner subject to such complete control by the prison authorities can ever consent voluntarily. The prisoner, after all, is deprived of his liberty and is very much dependent upon the prison staff if he is to obtain parole or even remission. Further, the prison authorities have great control over his quality of life in the prison; he can be isolated from other prisoners or punished in a variety of ways. Nonetheless, it would be quite wrong to say that prisoners could not give a voluntary consent under any circumstances. This would rob them of any decision-making authority over their own mind and body, and relegate them to the legal position of children. On the other hand it would be very naive not to recognise that great pressures exist in prison.

In *Freeman v Home Office* (1984) the Court of Appeal established the principle that a prisoner's consent is valid even though there are severe institutional restraints. In Mr Freeman's prison records it was shown repeatedly that he did not wish to receive major tranquillisers; the last entry read: 'consents reluctantly'. It is difficult to understand what a 'reluctant' consent is; it is quite possible that the consent was not truly free and that this was an instance where there may have been institutional constraints on his freedom of choice, but the Court of Appeal disagreed. It is suggested that, because of the undoubted institutional pressures on prisoners, extra care should be taken to ensure that consent to treatment is free and informed. Doctors in prisons are technically prison officers and responsible for discipline as well as treatment. No reasonable person would suggest that most doctors knowingly and intentionally use physical treatment as punishment. But there is a fine line between management and therapy and there are very great temptations to use 'treatment' to 'manage' particularly difficult patients.

Segregation

Segregation is a form of management in prisons where there is a blurred rationalisation between 'therapy' and 'control'. There are a number of different forms of segregation ('voluntary' segregation under rule 43, involuntary segregation under rule 43 or 48, and punitive segregation) which are surveyed elsewhere (Gostin and Staunton 1985). At highest risk of physical and psychological harm from the effects of segregation are mentally ill and mentally handicapped people. Isolation from people and environmental stimulation often exacerbates a person's mental disorder. Indeed, even in marginal cases isolation is known to result in symptoms of psychosis.

Segregation should only be used as a crisis intervention measure where a prisoner is about to cause imminent and substantial harm. Further minimum standards relating to conditions of confinement and a review of isolation should be established. There is a precedent for this in *A v the United Kingdom* (1980) where the European Commission on Human Rights agreed a friendly settlement between MIND and the UK for minimum standards of isolation at Broadmoor. 'A' had been isolated for five weeks in inhumane and degrading conditions without adequate space, ventilation, care, or association. The minimum standards agreed should be specifically enforceable and should include: the required amount of floor space and natural lighting; an individual programme of recreation, association, nursing care and treatment; clothing; mattresses and bedding; toilet and sanitation facilities; writing and reading materials; and the reception of visitors (see further Gostin and Staunton 1985 and Casales 1985).

Treatments which are experimental, hazardous or not fully established

Prisoners, because of their vulnerable position, are more likely to be subject to treatment which is experimental, hazardous or not fully established than virtually any other section of the population. In *Kaimowitz v Michigan* (1973) a US district court held that if experimental psycho-surgery was being used, it would be impossible for a prisoner to consent to it voluntarily. The *Kaimowitz* court set up an irrebuttable presumption that no prisoner can consent to experimental treatment because of the institutional pressures on him.

In this country, sex hormone implant treatments have been administered to prisoners. Prisoners effectively have little option but to acquiesce to such treatment because they sometimes face the sole alternative of an indefinite period of confinement in prison.

So far as *consent* to treatment is concerned, the solution in England and Wales lies in the Mental Health Act 1983 which states that any 'patient' (that is, any prisoner suffering or appearing to suffer from mental disorder (section 145)), even if he or she is 'not liable to be detained under this Act' (section 56(2)), cannot be given sex hormone implant treatment or psycho-surgery unless he or she consents; there must also be a multi-disciplinary review of the voluntariness and effectiveness of his or her consent; and a second doctor must state that treatment is beneficial. Given the very broad definition of 'patient' and of 'mental disorder' (that is, 'any other disorder or disability of mind' (section 1(2)), it is arguable that the 1983 Act applies to any prisoner to whom it is proposed to give any of these treatments. Even in those rare cases where the prison medical officers contend that the Mental Health Act does not apply, it would be expected that the courts would apply very strict standards in examining the voluntariness of consent in any case where treatment was unusually hazardous, experimental, or not fully established. In cases where the treatment is experimental in the sense that it is not for a therapeutic purpose, or there is a feasible alternative treatment of greater value or fewer risks, the courts could well adopt a *Kaimowitz*-type approach (For a more detailed examination of the consent to treatment provisions of the Mental Health Act and the common law, see Gostin 1985).

Medication for restraint or discipline

There may be times when treatment is sought to be used as a method of restraint, punishment or discipline. There are instances where sedatives are currently used to restrain prisoners. Here the prison authorities could argue that an injection is the least intrusive measure to prevent a prisoner from causing imminent harm. Alternatively, the use of tranquillisers over a long period of time may reduce aggression, and make the prisoner more cooperative and less disruptive. The medical profession, and their treatments, should never be used as a method of restraint or prevention in any of these ways. The practices of medicine and psychiatry are for the treatment of illness, and once the tools of medicine are used for punitive purposes (even where the end is arguably a just end) the legal, social and moral justifications for the practices cease to exist.

Court reports

It has already been pointed out that roughly half the prisoners classified as seriously mentally disordered by medical officers are unsentenced. It is a peculiarity of the British penal system that it has had the major responsibility for providing psychiatric reports for the courts. For many prisoners the court's insistence that a psychiatric assessment be carried out means that it must be made in custody, even if the prisoner is unlikely to receive a custodial sentence if found guilty. This is unfair, because a remand in custody for report is in effect a prison sentence without conviction which can last many months and, in some cases, for up to a year or more. Further, the fact that the person is imprisoned in foreign surroundings and no doubt upset by the experience makes it difficult to get a reliable psychiatric assessment (Zusman and Simon 1983). For lawyers there are additional doubts about assessment by prison medical officers. Many lawyers who deal with mental health cases consider that doctors working in closed establishments such as prisons or special hospitals are much more likely to recommend secure conditions as part of a custodial sentence than would, say, a general practitioner or a psychiatrist in a district general hospital or in a local mental hospital.

Some 8,000–9,000 reports are provided each year, a substantial burden on the Prison Medical Service. If the new system of remands for report under the Mental Health Act 1983 works well there should be an increasing use of NHS hospitals to obtain psychiatric reports for the courts. This could be a welcome trend which so far has not materialised. It is important that prisons and mental hospitals do not become places of custody for those who are not a real danger to the public. Wherever possible, psychiatric reports should be obtained while the person is on bail; if some custody is required, a remand to hospital would be the best alternative. Only rarely – where the person is highly dangerous and not seriously mentally disordered – should psychiatric reports continue to be given inside the prison system. The fact that most psychiatric reports to the courts are currently provided by prison doctors is an historical accident.

Justice, the strain on prisoners, and the quality of the reports, would all be improved by shifting responsibility for preparing reports from the prisons to the NHS.

Treatment of remand prisoners

In law, prisoners who are unconvicted but remanded in custody are entitled to full and equal access to the NHS. However, this does not occur in practice. Doctors who treat patients on remand are often prison medical officers; even the satisfactory system of joint appointments between the prisons and the NHS is being slowly phased out. Those who care for mentally disordered prisoners are usually prison officers with little or no training in the treatment and management of mental disorder. This has resulted in great suffering for mentally disordered people denied the kind of care they could expect in the NHS. (See Holloway case study page 50.)

All mentally disordered prisoners (and particularly those who are unsentenced) should be cared for and treated as are other patients in the best of the NHS. This means that the facilities, and the recreation, education, occupation and rehabilitation services must be as good as, say, those in the most advanced regional secure units; doctors must be primarily loyal to the NHS; and nurses must be trained and professionally registered in the care of mentally disordered people.

A proposal for amalgamation with the NHS

The Prison Medical Service is under great strain from overcrowding with mentally disordered prisoners, a lack of trained staff and a shortage of resources to provide the necessary care and treatment. Even if the courts took all possible steps to prevent seriously mentally disordered people going to prison, there will still be major problems for the foreseeable future. Some seriously mentally disordered people will continue to slip through the net and have to be treated and cared for in prison, while mentally vulnerable people – those with 'personality' disorders or those on the margins of mental disorder – may, as a matter of policy, remain in the prison system instead of going to mental hospitals. This leaves the Prison Medical Service with the daunting task of providing care in an essentially harsh and punitive environment which causes deterioration in mental health and self-esteem. Prisons are depressing, overcrowded and demoralising places with regimes which are rigid and sometimes cruel. Before going on to discuss possible remedies, it is worth examining some of the inherent weaknesses of the Prison Medical Service and why it has perennially been mistrusted as a 'caring' service.

It has already been pointed out that the prison doctor is a prison officer, managerially responsible to his senior. In matters of 'security' (which could be interpreted widely) the prison governor is senior to everyone at local level. Further, on matters of finance and general prison policy the final authority is non-medical and sometimes political. Any decision to introduce greater punishment through the use of seclusion or control units, or to withdraw the possibility of parole, can have powerful effects on a prisoner's mental health. Since overall resource allocation is not the responsibility of the Prison Medical Service, it has been possible for more and more money to be spent on 'security' and less on medical services, which are often seen as a 'soft' approach to crime. Any medical practitioner working for the Home Office is likely to be frustrated and confused, because the primary aim of the Home Secretary is not the health of prisoners but security and law and order in the community. Prison doctors, therefore, have a dual loyalty – to the state and to the patient – and there are very great pressures to favour the state when there is a conflict (Bowden 1978). From the prisoner's perspective, the doctor is too often simply the facilitator of the process of control, management and punishment.

One instance of this is the duty of medical officers to certify prisoners as 'fit for punishment'. The prison system puts the doctor in a bind. If he certifies that some prisoners are fit for harsh treatment, such as solitary confinement which causes psychiatric problems, then he is seen in the eyes of the prisoners and of society as merely colluding in a repressive system. Yet, if he fails to certify a seriously mentally ill prisoner as unfit, the punishment would have unconscionable effects. The fact that the prison doctor owes his employment allegiance to the prison system does not help him to take a principled and independent stand on the use of punishment.

The quality of staff required in the Prison Medical Service to provide the care and treatment needed by mentally vulnerable prisoners must be exceedingly high. Again, there are problems. The Prison Medical Service is isolated and unattractive and, consequently, recruitment is a major difficulty (Home Office 1964). Nurses in the Prison Medical Service are not trained psychiatric nurses and cannot attend recognised courses on psychiatric nursing in a secure environment. Also, a system of exchanges between prison hospital officers and the NHS cannot be developed because hospital officers are subject to different conditions of employment from NHS nurses. There are at present very few formal links between hospital officers and the NHS (Parliamentary All-Party Penal Affairs Group 1982).

The two major structural problems in the Prison Medical Service are caused by its direct accountability to the Home Office and its isolation from the NHS, which make recruitment and training of high quality staff difficult. The physical and mental health problems of prisoners are essentially the same as the rest of the population, and certainly no less severe. The training and experience needed to combat these problems lie primarily in the NHS. A prisoner, simply because he is deprived of his liberty, should not also be deprived of the right to care under the service. Indeed, many prisoners have serious forms of mental disorders, such as schizophrenia and severe mental handicap. They should be transferred to the NHS but the isolation of the Prison Medical Service makes this very difficult.

The failure to incorporate the Prison Medical Service in the NHS when it was introduced in 1948 was regrettable, and should be corrected. The Prison Medical Service should become a part of the National Health Service, with the responsibility for health services in prisons under the control of the district health authority. The authority is responsible for all health services in its district and the local prison population should be no exception. Since the DHA has a statutory duty to meet all reasonable health care needs it would be expected to devote a fair share of its resources to the fundamental mental health problems manifested in the prison system. Its control of hospitals in the district, under the overall responsibility of the regional health authority, should ease the problem of finding beds for prisoners who need to be transferred to mental hospitals. There is important support for such a proposal from the Royal College of Psychiatrists (1979) (but see Gunn 1985).

The Prison Department (Home Office 1982) is vehemently opposed to this proposal, arguing that the Home Secretary is accountable to Parliament for the provision of prison medical services; that the Prison Medical Service is subject to supervision by the Inspectorate of Prisons; and that prisoners can make complaints to the Parliamentary Commissioner. The department said: 'If the Prison Medical

Service were incorporated into the National Health Service it would not be possible to devise arrangements by which there would be the same degree of central control and ministerial accountability for medical services in establishments ... The present system of control and accountability provides an essential safeguard for those in custody'. This argument is wholly unconvincing because there are already equally strong systems of accountability in the NHS, with ministerial responsibility given to the Secretary of State for Social Services and a complaints procedure through the Health Service Commissioner. To have doctors, nurses and occupational therapists from an independent NHS accountable to their own Secretary of State would help counteract the insular attitude caused by working in closed prison establishments. Complete centralisation of relatively secret institutions is unhealthy and leads to suspicion; the safeguards provided by an independent NHS would surely provide better protection for prisoners.

The Prison Department also argues that the medical officer's role is not only clinical; it also involves advising prison officer colleagues about 'activities which can go well beyond the normal boundaries of nursing care'. These duties are not clearly specified. If they are concerned with hygiene and living conditions or giving support to people who are mentally unfit, the tasks could be carried out equally well by GPs and other doctors. Should these duties mean giving advice about control, management and punishment, there is an even greater need for a voice from outside the system.

An alternative to full amalgamation would be to make the Prison Medical Service a special health authority under the National Health Service Act 1977 (Gunn 1985). This would place a positive duty on the prison authorities to meet all reasonable requirements for medical care by using outside contractors to provide much of the service (Gostin and Staunton 1985). There are precedents; dental treatment is provided under the NHS scheme and education officers employed by local authorities run courses in prisons. The expertise of an independent service with its own career structure and status, and a system of accountability to the NHS, can be applied to prisoners, even though they are confined.

This solution would not solve the problem of inequality of access to health service care; but at least it would ensure that the provision of medical services to prisoners would be the responsibility of the DHSS, which is separate from the Prison Department and not concerned with matters of order, discipline and security which often conflict with the therapeutic responsibilities of doctors, nurses and other professionals in the NHS.

The major disadvantage of this proposal is that a special health authority, practically speaking, would have to be constituted nationally, preventing a system of accountability at local level.

Whichever option is chosen – the *status quo*, full amalgamation, or a special health authority – it is clear that prisons will continue to be receptacles for people with chronic psychiatric problems. Therefore, it is essential that government recognises this and devotes much more resources, time and expertise to the provision of treatment, nursing and other care. In particular, mentally disordered prisoners must have the same right of access to medical care as NHS patients. Those who treat and care for them must be NHS doctors and nurses and not, as at present, prison doctors and prison officers who are often completely untrained in mental health care. The problems are so complex that an official working party should be set up, comprising distinguished health professionals, administrators and policymakers with the task of devising a formula for the transformation of psychiatric services in prisons. Provision needs to be made for 'psychopaths' and other people with 'personality disorders' who will be increasingly sent to prison rather than hospital. These offenders could benefit from a therapeutic community and group psychotherapy (on a truly consenting basis), as provided at Grendon and Barlinnie. Thought will need to be given to helping people with alcohol or drug dependence, or with epilepsy; to those who are vulnerable and need asylum, and the mentally ill or mentally handicapped. Society can no longer close its eyes to these immense social problems or ignore the fact that many of our most vulnerable people – for good or bad reasons – often end up in prisons, detention centres and youth custody.

Holloway Prison: a case study

C1, Holloway Prison's unit for mentally disturbed women, was opened in 1977. It has integral accommodation for 56 women in 36 single cells and four 5-bedded dormitories. C1 is a medical unit, supervised by a senior prison medical officer and staffed by prison officers and nurses. It provides a characteristic, albeit powerful, illustration of the problems of caring for severely mentally disturbed people in the Prison Medical Service. It houses the most disturbed women in the prison system; three quarters are diagnosed as mentally ill, with a preponderance of schizophrenia, depression and personality disorder. Women's reactions to confinement are different from that of men, with a particular tendency to self-harm which demands adequate facilities and sensitive care and treatment. Almost half the women in C1 were thought to have suicidal tendencies or to be at risk from self-harm. They are often vulnerable and isolated with some 42 per cent having no contact outside the prison (Stuart and Shine 1984).

NCCL and MIND have launched a campaign for adequate and humane care and treatment of women in C1. Much of the evidence for this case study is from the policy document written for the campaign (Bingley and Gostin 1985). The Home Office Holloway Project Committee report, published in July 1985, made extensive recommendations about C1, including its replacement by a purpose-built unit.

Medical assessment for remand prisoners

Stuart and Shine (1984) showed that over 90 per cent of prisoners in C1 were on remand – 40 per cent unconvicted and 51 per cent convicted awaiting sentence. Nearly three quarters had been remanded for medical reports. When the cases came to court nearly 60 per cent resulted in dismissal, granting of bail or non-custodial sentences. Another 25 per cent resulted in hospital orders.

These figures are significant for they show a group of women prisoners who have, by and large, been determined by the courts as not requiring custodial sentences. From moral, social and legal perspectives they are in the same position as any human being deserving the high standard of health care provided in the best of the NHS.

1 *Bail*
It follows that wherever possible these women should not be remanded in custody but granted bail and placed informally in a mental hospital or clinic for medical assessment and/or treatment. This is well within the powers of the court and should be considered more often than it is, sparing the women the sometimes traumatic ordeal of confinement. Evidence that bail is a feasible alternative lies in the final disposal of cases where the same women either are not convicted or are given non-custodial sentences.

2 *Remand to hospital for report or treatment*
In cases where bail is inappropriate women can be remanded to hospital under section 37 or 38 of the Mental Health Act 1983,

either for medical report or for treatment. The fact that 25 per cent of those placed in custody at Holloway were later given hospital orders clearly suggests that there are cases where therapeutic remands to hospital should be considered. Information received from staff at Holloway suggests that hospitals have not always been helpful in admitting remand cases under the 1983 Act, and that the Act has not relieved the pressure on Holloway to function as a medical assessment unit. Hospital managers, consultants and nurses in the NHS must think hard before turning down these cases; it can mean cruel and inhumane prison confinement for the most severely ill and vulnerable women in our society. Courts must also be prepared to press the point whenever necessary.

Staffing and design

Holloway Prison has had a chronic shortage of staff and has been unable to overcome the problems caused by staff refusing to work overtime. The design of C1 provides very limited space for association, recreation or occupation. As a result of inadequate staffing and constricted design the regime is highly restrictive, with prisoners often being locked in their small rooms for 23 hours a day. Some rooms are stripped bare and highly insanitary. Staffing is also provided by prison officers with an understanding of control and discipline but little knowledge of mental health nursing. There are some trained nurses but far too few to meet the needs of prisoners.

Treatment

Holloway has one of the highest rates of psychotropic drug use in the prison system. In 1982/83 the rate was 365 doses per prisoner or one dose per prisoner for every day of the year. There are no separate figures for C1 but as a psychiatric unit it must constitute a substantial portion of the whole.

Medical and theological reports received by MIND show the unit to be highly inhumane with conditions which exacerbate the mental state of prisoners. Enforced segregation, sometimes for long periods, the lack of medical or nursing attention, and the confined conditions, produce a regime which is not only far inferior to most NHS hospitals but inhumane and degrading, possibly to an extent that violates basic international standards, such as those under article 3 of the European Convention of Human Rights.

No one can establish a precise connection between the restrictive, inhumane regime and severe physical harm to prisoners. Nevertheless, there has been a worrying number of deaths and self-mutilations in C1 over the last four years.

Proposals

1 *Assessment be provided in NHS or court clinics*

NCCL and MIND conclude that the assessment of all mentally disordered women should be carried out in the NHS. In the USA, for example, courts have their own psychiatric assessment clinics so that no mentally disordered person need be sent to prison for a report. The clinics, staffed entirely by experienced medical personnel, are for medical assessment. They are accountable to the courts and derive their funding from the court system.

2 *Equality in treatment between mentally disordered prisoners and patients*

One of the principles enshrined in Britain is the right of equal access to medical and nursing care of good quality. This concept is particularly significant when it is remembered that 90 per cent of prisoners at C1 are unsentenced. The optimum way of upholding this principle is by providing care in the NHS through bail or remands to hospital (see above). In the short term it is recognised that some mentally disordered people will be medically assessed and treated in prison, requiring the development of new facilities with staffing, design and treatment equal to the best in the NHS.

3 *Accountability*

The responsibility of the Mental Health Act Commission to keep under review the rights of detained patients in hospital could be extended fruitfully to prisoners undergoing treatment for mental disorder.

Summary of recommendations: Mentally disordered people in the prison system

Unsentenced Prisoners

1 *An unsentenced person should rarely be remanded in custody for the purposes of a psychiatric report, and never in cases where a conviction would not result in a custodial sentence. Nor should an unsentenced*

person be remanded to prison if it would cause a deterioration in his mental condition.

a) *An unsentenced person should, wherever possible, be released on bail for psychiatric assessment;*

b) *if he is immediately dangerous, he should be remanded to hospital for assessment or treatment;*

c) *if these proposals cannot be implemented quickly, the interim remand prisoners should be cared for and treated by NHS doctors and nurses, which is their right.*

Consent to treatment

2 *A prisoner should not be given treatment without his informed consent, free of improper threats or inducements.*

3 *Minimum prison standards should be established (particularly for segregation) which are clear and specifically enforceable by an independent authority.*

4 *Psychotropic drugs or other treatments should never be used in the management of the prison.*

Amalgamation of the Prison Medical Service with the National Health Service

5 *The Prison Medical Service should become a part of the National Health Service with district health authorities responsible for prison medical services and accountable to regional health authorities.*

6 *As an alternative, the Prison Medical Service should be made into a special health authority, directly accountable to the Secretary of State for Social Services. NHS professionals should provide all care and treatment for mentally disordered prisoners.*

Additional resources needed

7 *Whichever option is chosen – the status quo, full amalgamation, or the establishment of a special health authority – the government must devote considerably more resources to the treatment and care of mentally disordered persons in prisons.*

8 *Because of the complexity of the problem of providing care and treatment for so many people with diverse forms of mental vulnerability, an official working party should be established to devise a set of proposals for changing the provision of mental health services for mentally disordered prisoners.*

Holloway case study

9 **Medical assessment** *or treatment of prisoners should take place in the NHS, not in prison. This can be accomplished either by the use of bail when appropriate; or by the use of remands to hospital for report or treatment under the Mental Health Act 1983.*

10 **Equity in treatment** *Mentally disordered prisoners should have the same access to health care of the quality available to everyone else in the best of the NHS.*

11 **Accountability** *The Mental Health Act Commission should have jurisdiction to review the care of mentally disordered prisoners.*

CHAPTER THREE

Special hospitals

Defined

The Secretary of State for Social Services has a duty under section 4 of the National Health Service Act 1977 'to provide and maintain establishments . . . for persons subject to detention under the Mental Health Act 1983 who in his opinion require treatment under conditions of special security on account of their dangerous, violent or criminal propensities'. The hospitals established under section 4 are called special hospitals; the four in existence are Broadmoor, Rampton, Moss Side and Park Lane.

'Subject to detention'

The definition in section 4 of the 1977 Act suggests that special hospitals can only be used for patients liable to detention under the Mental Health Act. There have been a few cases where informal patients have been kept for a time in the special hospitals – for example, after a Mental Health Review Tribunal has discharged a patient from being liable to be detained. Continued residence in a special hospital was with the patient's consent and for a period limited to finding accommodation in the community (which sometimes can be very long). As at 31 December 1984 there were three informal patients resident in a special hospital, all at Park Lane. This use of special hospitals was not envisaged in the 1977 Act, and if an informal patient were to remain for an extended period of time in a special hospital it would cause concern because of the closed conditions in which all special hospital patients must be kept. It is recommended that only patients liable to detention should remain in a special hospital. There are too many pressures on patients to consent, and if no meaningful alternative is offered there is no real choice. Further, special hospitals are maximum security institutions which in principle should not house informal patients.

'Special security'

The term 'special security' in section 4 of the 1977 Act has been construed as meaning that it should not be less secure than that required for the most dangerous (category 'A') prisoners (House of Commons Estimates Committee 1968). In practice, the security in special hospitals is preserved by a secure perimeter wall, locked wards, the vigilance of staff and a system of constant checks. The security precautions, however, are not designed to prevent an organised and well planned attempt from outside to enable a patient to escape. The interests of security and those of treatment sometimes conflict, and reduced security may be a consequence of increased treatment and rehabilitation programmes. It is suggested that special hospitals should provide 'flexible' security so that patients who require more intensive rehabilitation should be able to have more freedom and greater opportunity for leave of absence for shopping visits, family holidays and so on. This is a proposal which most special hospitals are already beginning to implement by introducing systems of 'parole', where some patients can have freer opportunities to walk in the hospital grounds and go on leave of absence and shopping trips.

'Dangerous, violent or criminal propensities'

Only patients who have 'dangerous, violent or criminal propensities' should be detained in a special hospital. It would appear that if a patient clearly does not meet these criteria it would be unlawful to detain him in a special hospital. Yet a special hospital research report observed that in 10 per cent of its sample, patients were admitted to special hospitals in spite of the Secretary of State's view that they did not require conditions of special security. Further, some eight per cent of the population of special hospitals had been approved for transfer or discharge by the Secretary of State, indicating that they also, in his opinion, did not require conditions of special security (Dell 1980). The position, moreover, is not improving. At the end of 1984, 233 patients were awaiting transfer to local NHS hospitals or to the Eastdale unit, an increase of 20 per cent on the 1982 figure (see page 75 and 76).

In *Ashingdane's* case, a patient's transfer from Broadmoor Hospital (recommended by the RMO and consented to by the Secretary of State for Social Services and the Home Secretary) was prevented by COHSE who had maintained an absolute ban on admission to Oakwood Hospital of any patient subject to restrictions on discharge. The patient was prevented from suing the Secretary of State and the health authority because of section 141 of the Mental

Health Act 1959.* The situation arose, therefore, where a patient not considered dangerous was detained in a high security mental hospital against medical and other advice; and he was not able to put that point to a court of law. The European Court of Human Rights (*Ashingdane v the United Kingdom 1985*) recently upheld the restrictions placed on Mr Ashingdane's access to the courts but was critical of the inflexibility of the NHS in not being able to ensure his prompt transfer to a local hospital.

Patients who are not of 'dangerous, violent or criminal propensities' should not be detained in a special hospital. Mental Health Review Tribunals should have the power to *direct* the transfer of any patient who does not meet the statutory criteria. Special hospitals were built as maximum security establishments for highly dangerous patients. They significantly restrict a person's freedom and quality of life. Detention of such patients should not be seen solely as an 'administrative' issue in the sense that a local hospital bed cannot be found. Rather it is a 'liberty' issue which should involve the patient having certain basic rights. Such rights can be enforced only by giving a tribunal or other appropriate body the right to compel admission where there are strong grounds for a transfer.

Management

The special hospitals are administered centrally by the Secretary of State for Social Services. He has direct control of, and managerial responsibilities for, the special hospitals; special hospitals are not administered locally by regional or district health authorities as are other NHS hospitals. Indeed there is a common, but incorrect, belief that the special hospitals are not part of the NHS. In fact the special hospitals are part of the NHS and are provided for under the same Act as the rest of the health service; indeed one special hospital (Rampton) is managed by a special health authority (see below). By section 145(1) of the Mental Health Act 1983, the Secretary of State for Social Services is designated as the manager of the special hospitals. Administrative functions vested in the Secretary of State are exercised by a central management body within the department of

---

* Section 141 of the 1959 Act – now section 139 of the 1983 Act – requires patients to get permission from the High Court before they can bring civil proceedings against a person acting under the Mental Health Act; and the High Court will not give permission unless the person to be proceeded against has acted in bad faith or without reasonable care.

Health and Social Security called the 'Office Committee for the Special Hospitals'.

The Secretary of State has power to direct a regional, district or special health authority to exercise on his behalf management functions relating to special hospitals. The Secretary of State has made such a direction only in relation to Rampton Hospital. A special health authority known as the Rampton Hospital Review Board manages the hospital in almost all respects except in relation to the power to make admission decisions and the appointment of staff, which the Secretary of State still retains.

The four special hospitals

On 31 December 1984 the special hospitals had a resident population of 1,569 patients; the trend is downwards (DHSS 1985). The special hospital system is organised on a national basis without formal geographic catchment areas, although some attempt is made to take into account the normal residence of a patient. All special hospitals may admit patients classified under any of the four categories of mental disorder, but for historical reasons each has developed differently: Broadmoor and Park Lane are primarily for mentally ill and psychopathic patients, while both Rampton and Moss Side take a significant number of mentally impaired patients.

There follows a description of the development of the four special hospitals which seeks to show why there is little room for complacency in finding solutions to the problems they pose to the mental health service.

Broadmoor Hospital

Broadmoor Hospital, situated in Crowthorne, Berkshire, was originally opened in 1863 as a criminal lunatic asylum run by the Home Office; it was built with convict labour. Management was taken over by the Board of Control in 1948 and by the Ministry of Health in 1959. A chronicle of Broadmoor has been published dealing with its development up to 1952 (Partridge 1953; see also Cohen 1981; Hamilton 1985).

There has been a long line of critical reports on Broadmoor Hospital from the House of Commons Estimates Committee (1968), the Butler committee (Home Office 1974), the NHS Hospital Advisory Service (1975), the Parliamentary All-Party Mental Health

Group (1980) and the European Commission of Human Rights (*B v the United Kingdom*).

Rampton Hospital and the Eastdale Unit

Rampton, situated in Retford, Nottinghamshire, was opened in 1910 as a criminal lunatic asylum owned by the Home Office; the management passed to the Board of Control and then to the Ministry of Health in 1959. A description of the functioning of Rampton prior to 1960 was provided by Street and Tong (1960). In 1971 a team from the NHS Hospital Advisory Service prepared a report and in 1973 the Elliot report was completed. On 22 May 1979 the Yorkshire Television film, 'Secret Hospital', was screened; it contained many serious allegations of ill-treatment of patients by staff. The allegations were referred to the Director of Public Prosecutions who arranged for a police investigation, and a review of the 'organisation, management and functioning' of the hospital was initiated. The Rampton review team (DHSS 1980a) (chaired by Sir John Boynton) reported in 1980; its principal recommendation was the establishment of a review board. The board, chaired by Mr Leslie Teeman, was established in July 1981 and presented its first report to the Secretary of State in October 1982, and its second report a year later. (Rampton Review Board 1982, 1983). Its third report was submitted to the Secretary of State early in 1985.

The Eastdale Unit at Balderton Hospital was opened in May 1974 and provides accommodation for male patients discharged from the special hospitals, particularly for Rampton patients. The unit, which has 30 beds, provides rehabilitation facilities for an average of six months with a view to transfer to a local hospital or discharge into the community. The Trent Regional Health Authority (1982) recommended other units of this kind, and this proposal should be supported and carried out. Units to help the rehabilitation and resocialisation of special hospital patients are urgently required. This is illustrated by the fact that as at July 1984 there were 12 patients awaiting admission to the Eastdale Unit, four from Broadmoor and eight from Rampton (Parliamentary debates 1984c). Clearly there is a need for more beds in units like Eastdale.

Moss Side Hospital

Moss Side, situated in Maghull, Lancashire, was purchased by the Board of Control in 1914; taken over by the War Office and opened in 1919; it was re-opened in 1920 under lease to the Ministry of Pensions for use as an epileptic colony. In 1933 it was re-opened as a state institution for mental defectives; ownership was vested in the Ministry of Health in 1946. It became a special hospital in 1959.

There is very little known publicly about Moss Side as there have been no major published studies or reports into its practices. The major difficulty facing staff at Moss Side is the transfer of patients. As at July 1984 the hospital had 49 patients on the transfer list, the majority of whom have been waiting for more than a year (Parliamentary debates 1984b). The number of beds it provides is small and is decreasing. As at 31 December 1983 it had 271 patients, a number that has decreased since then to about 235. As at July 1984, there were 49 patients (between 20 and 25 per cent of the entire population) awaiting transfer, more than half of whom had been waiting for over a year. (Seven have been waiting 2–3 years and three for 3–4 years.)

Children in the special hospitals

One of the major concerns at Moss Side is that over the years it has taken children and young persons, sometimes as young as 11 and 12, although it has none at present. Admission to a high security mental hospital can be extremely detrimental to a young person. At Moss Side young people had been removed from family or parent-figures, losing most of their association with other children. They were sometimes subject to seclusion, physical restraint and potentially high doses of drugs, and they suffered the life-long stigma of having been detained in a special hospital.

MIND represented one young person who was featured in the television documentary 'Life for Christine' in 1981. At the age of 15 she was admitted to Moss Side. A mental health tribunal heard expert evidence that she was so heavily drugged, and detained for so many years, that her health was severely endangered. An independent doctor diagnosed that she was suffering from a potentially irreversible condition called tardive dyskinesia which involves uncontrollable shaking of the limbs.

Around the same time, MIND was also representing a young girl aged 15 at Broadmoor. She was secluded for long periods in a room without furniture, without access to her ordinary clothes or an opportunity for association; she was even stripped of her hearing aid and glasses. She was said to have had a tantrum and knocked over a

61

case of books in her room; this was the reason for her seclusion. When seen in seclusion by her representative she was sitting on the floor, quiet and depressed. There was no indication that she might be imminently dangerous to herself or others.

Staff in the special hospitals are acutely aware of all of these difficulties in admitting young patients; they try extremely hard to protect them. Yet as a policy matter it is wrong to place any child or young person in a special hospital and it is suggested that only patients over the age of 18 should be eligible for admission. As at 31 December 1984 there were ten patients aged 16 or 17 in the special hospitals. Currently, none is below the age of 16 (direct personal communication with the DHSS, 28 February 1985).

Park Lane Hospital

Park Lane is the newest special hospital and is built adjacent to Moss Side, with which it shares some facilities. An advance unit with 70 male patients transferred from Broadmoor Hospital was opened in 1974; the first 100 beds were made available in September 1980. The hospital was officially opened in 1984, and on completion will contain 410 beds for mental illness and psychopathic disorder. As yet, there are no female patients. The facilities are extremely good and nurses maintain a more informal atmosphere than at Broadmoor. But it is too soon to provide any judgments about the treatment and care.

Before examining some of the critical content of the reports into the special hospitals it is important to stress that there are many positive aspects, and there have been substantial improvements since the 1970s. The facilities available (particularly at Broadmoor and Park Lane) are exceptionally good, so there is a higher staff–patient ratio than at most mental hospitals and a wide range of occupational therapies and opportunities for education. Many of the problems of special hospitals do not stem from any lack of expertise or compassion among the staff, but from their location, physical plant, history and traditions. The staff are faced with the daunting problem of having to provide maximum security conditions in hospitals that have national catchment areas and facilities built in the Victorian age. Indeed, given the obstacles, professional staff have achieved remarkably well. They have responded with resilience to the criticisms in the 1970s and made substantial gains in standards since then. Most of the observations below are drawn from reports on the special hospitals, from correspondence with patients, and from visits to the hospitals.

Security and custodial attitudes

Security in the special hospitals, particularly Broadmoor and Rampton, is extensive and clearly visible. The NHS Hospital Advisory Service (1975) report on Broadmoor gives an accurate description which is still true. 'Locked doors, a perimeter wall, checking of patients in and out; nursing staff wear a dark blue uniform with a peaked cap; patients' letters are subject to censor, and visiting is carefully controlled'.

It is clearly important that there should be a well thought out plan for security. However, some special hospitals are able to achieve good security without it being so visible and obtrusive. By having good perimeter security, Park Lane is able to dispense with much of the regimentation and restrictions which are obvious in hospitals like Broadmoor and Rampton. Broadmoor has, to its credit, a long tradition of parole so that some patients (probably far too few) are able to walk inside the grounds. Rampton has not had a system of parole but now has a new perimeter fence and will introduce a parole system shortly.

The Prison Officers Association

Most nurses in the special hospitals are not members of the Royal College of Nursing or of any NHS union, but are members of the Prison Officers Association. It is strongly advised that nurses should have their sole loyalty to psychiatric nursing, shown by their membership of a professional association or a health service union, in their dress and in their training, experience and actions. It is worth noting, for example, that staff at Park Lane do not wear uniforms. The patients and staff agree that this promotes a better atmosphere. Nurses at Broadmoor and Rampton still wear blue prison uniforms and peaked caps.

The conflict between nursing care and security is perhaps most acute at Rampton. The first annual report of the Rampton Review Board (1982) stated:

We have had setbacks following the outcome of court trials and have experienced industrial action restricting resocialisation activities for patients. This has included refusals to provide escorts, refusals to allow weekend assessment visits for patients which are necessary for them to secure hostel/hospital places and prevention of patient working parties outside the secure perimeter of the hospital. The POA were asked to stop their industrial action. Unfortunately, their cooperation was not forthcoming and further restrictions were imposed (*The Guardian* 1985).

To the credit of the Rampton Review Board, they have now had these restrictions lifted. But any industrial action in the special hospitals affects human beings, and the industrial strength and lingering custodial attitudes of the POA are still present. At Rampton, for example, nurses have been in conflict with management for barring visits on the wards. The ban was introduced following the Yorkshire Television programme 'Secret Hospital' in 1979. The Rampton Review Board ordered an end to the ban in February 1985. This provoked the accusation from the chairman of the POA at Rampton that 'communication between management and staff is virtually nil'.

Management in the special hospitals has challenged nurses to maintain high professional standards, and they must be supported in this endeavour. Rampton nurses deserve credit for winning back the approval of the Royal College of Nursing to have nurse training reintroduced at the hospital. The training is in conjunction with the health authority. Such joint training programmes are to be welcomed and developed further.

The re-building programme: level of expenditure

For many years there was severe overcrowding in the special hospitals, especially Broadmoor and Rampton. Broadmoor was built to house 500 patients but in 1975 the total was 763; it is now just over 500. The overcrowding has been alleviated by an ambitious programme of re-building and by transfer of patients to Park Lane.

The level of increased expenditure over the past five years in the special hospitals is remarkable. The four hospitals have benefited from a 47 per cent increase in health spending at a time when the NHS has faced retrenchment and cuts in services. Despite a fall in the number of special hospital patients from 2,028 in 1979 to 1,569 by the end of 1984, the DHSS ordered a rapid increase in expenditure from £15 million to over £40 million during that period. Plans are also well advanced for a £15 million development at Broadmoor, and feasibility studies are being undertaken for a full refurbishment of Rampton.

It is to be regretted that the DHSS sought to relieve these problems by spending more money on refurbishing and expanding the special hospitals. It is, of course, essential to provide more humane and private conditions for patients and to make special hospitals cleaner and safer places to live – for example, by increasing and improving bathing and toilet facilities and making better arrangements and facilities for fire precautions. However, very substantial funds poured into these hospitals to re-build them on site hinder sensible policy discussions about the best way of providing treatment for patients in secure conditions. Even if special hospitals are not completely phased out, there is a strong and continuing case for the relocation of many of their patients. Adoption of sensible policies should mean that special hospitals would exist in a different form, with far fewer patients, than at present. It should be observed, moreover, that much of the money spent on special hospitals has been badly needed to provide secure provision in local hospitals (see Chapter 4).

Rehabilitation

For the great majority of patients the most important task in preparing them for their return to less secure conditions and, eventually, to their homes in the community, is rehabilitation – that is, the process of enabling a patient to retain or build up competence to live in the community.

This is the greatest single difficulty in the special hospital system. The concept of rehabilitation requires mental health professionals to 'test out' how a patient will react under increasingly less secure and less controlled conditions. There are a whole variety of tasks, activities and relationships which the patient must be able to come to terms with if he is ever to be released as a healthier, safer person. These range from shopping, knowing about money and making everyday decisions, to how to relate with friends, family and employer. Most of the staff in special hospitals now recognise the importance of rehabilitation. But given the national catchment areas of special hospitals, rehabilitation is difficult to achieve. A person may be hundreds of miles from the community where he will live when he is discharged, and can easily lose contact with those people who should be most important in helping him to rebuild his life.

Further, because special hospitals must be secure enough to contain the most determined absconders and the most dangerous people, it is only possible to give patients a certain amount of freedom and autonomy. The environment of the special hospitals is severe and restrictive for the patient. This kind of régime does not ultimately best protect the public because there is relatively little opportunity to judge how patients will react to more autonomy and freedom; or, for example, how a patient might react to alcohol or a relationship with a wife or girlfriend. Frankly, doctors have little idea how a patient will behave outside the restrictive confines of the special hospital. This means that a highly controlled psychopath may seem reasonably safe inside a special hospital but be dangerous or relapse when transferred to the open conditions of a local hospital or discharged into the community with little or no supervision or aftercare.

There is also a residual distrust of the concept of rehabilitation that almost every report into the special hospitals has referred to. The NHS Hospital Advisory Service report on Broadmoor (1975) said: 'It is a fact that Broadmoor staff in general view rehabilitation with some suspicion. They equate it with certain policies which are welcome in an open hospital, but which are incompatible with Broadmoor'. The HAS report concluded that there is 'no evidence of a coordinated rehabilitation policy for the hospital'. The Elliot (1973) and Boynton reports (DHSS 1980a) on Rampton came to very similar conclusions. Dr John Hamilton (1985) has shown similar concern: 'Criticisms made by the Elliot Report on Rampton in 1973 and the Hospital Advisory Service on Broadmoor in 1975 of the lack of effective rehabilitation policies are to a large extent still unanswered.'

More recently the Trent RHA (1982) and the Rampton Review Board (1983) also expressed reservations about the priority given to rehabilitation at Rampton.

Constructing the patient's day

The major strength of the special hospital system is in the high quality and range of occupational and recreational activities available to patients. At Broadmoor, more than 50 per cent of all patients attend occupational therapy during the day. This is an achievement which must be encouraged. But the problems for the rest of the patients who are not able to attend regularly any activity outside the ward were illustrated in the case of *B v the United*

Kingdom before the European Commission of Human Rights. The patient had spent over three years without any occupational or recreational placement, remaining virtually all the time on the same ward without active treatment or occupation. He had seen his doctor for less than fifteen minutes in over four years at the hospital, and had not received any other form of treatment – either physical or psychotherapeutic. It was suggested that he was in receipt of 'milieu therapy' – that is, his mere presence on the ward was therapeutic. Given that the Commission found the conditions lacked privacy and the rudiments of sanitation and health, the claim of 'milieu therapy' sounds hollow.

The way that a patient's day is constructed is extremely important to his quality of life in any hospital. If he stays on the ward he will become bored and lose initiative, and his will to re-train and socialise will be diminished. Rampton has made great improvements in the number of patients going to recreational or occupational facilities during the day. But there is one major problem which was emphasised in the Boynton report (DHSS 1980a) and still not solved four years on. It is that nursing staff work a twelve-hour shift for only a few days a week. This causes management problems because staff after such a long day are unlikely to be at their most patient and sensitive to the needs of residents. It also encourages staff to work overtime (extra days), which is expensive and managerially untenable. Most important of all, it means that the patient's day must centre around the shifts of the staff so that many patients are forced to go to bed at or before 8 pm and to stay in their rooms until 8 am the next day. The hospital management team has introduced a 'twilight' shift so that a minority of patients can now stay up later. The review board is reluctant to impose needed changes because of the powerful financial and social incentives of the current shift system.

Institutionalisation

The danger of institutionalisation is particularly severe in special hospitals. The high security environment, which involves marching, head counting and confinement in small quarters for long periods, contributes to institutional dependence.

The danger of institutionalisation is heightened where there is a high proportion of long-term chronic patients. It is staggering to consider that over 50 per cent of the residents have been detained in a special hospital for over five years and five per cent have been detained for 20 years or more. All the special hospitals have a powerful and effective social conditioning process.

Once a person enters a special hospital the effects on his life are profound, and certainly much worse than admission to a prison, youth custody or any other institution. He is likely to be detained longer for identical crimes; the stigma is enormous and continuing; and he can receive treatment against his will (see below). A Park Lane patient was recently discharged from hospital after his doctor and a Mental Health Review Tribunal said he was entirely sane. The patient wrote a letter to the NCCL saying that since release no one would have anything to do with him because, as an ex-special hospital patient, he was 'tainted'. His family and friends shunned him and no one would give him a job or rent him a flat. Indeed it is difficult to find many ex-special hospital patients who claim that their time at a special hospital was a therapeutic and useful experience (Cohen 1981).

Treatment

Because the special hospitals are so secretive it is extremely difficult to know the extent of abuses of compulsory treatment. Yet there have been well documented examples, particularly in relation to certain consultants. There is an ethical committee at Broadmoor which is chaired by a senior academic at Oxford University. A similar arrangement has just been instituted at Rampton. But these ethical committees do not review matters which come under the extremely wide purview of 'clinical judgment', and even when an ethical committee makes a recommendation contrary to the view of a consultant, it has no power to enforce the recommendation. Moreover, because its position is so tenuous, and reliant upon the continued goodwill of the hospital, the ethical committee never allows the public to know its concerns about the hospital. Some other special hospitals have no ethical committee. All special hospitals should have ethical committees to consider not only research proposals but treatment issues affecting the interests of patients.

The three most documented potential misuses of treatment concern medication, unmodified ECT and seclusion and restraint which came to light on one ward at Broadmoor in 1980. The dosages of major tranquillisers for every patient on that ward exceeded the maximum recommendation by the manufacturer by a factor of two and in some cases by much more. There were no questions asked nor any independent review as it was said the matter was entirely one for the doctors' clinical judgment.

At about the same time, ECT had been given by the same consultant in an unmodified form – that is, without muscle relaxants or anaesthetics. Unmodified ECT is not used any more in modern psychiatry because it can result in major fractures and cause the patient grave physical harm. When the allegation was first made it was denied by the DHSS and Broadmoor. Shortly after the Parliamentary All-Party Mental Health Group (1980) was told that it had indeed occurred three times in one year, each time by the same consultant.

Patrick Jenkin, then Secretary of State, replied to a complaint from MIND as follows (27 March 1980): 'As regards the use of unmodified ECT, I do not see this as in any sense a matter of professional misconduct but rather as an important clinical issue' (MIND 1980).

The use of seclusion at the special hospitals first came to the public's attention through the European Commission of Human Rights. In *A v the United Kingdom* (1980) a Broadmoor patient, who was one of several suspected of starting a fire, was secluded in a small room for over five weeks. He was virtually unable to leave the room except to clean his plastic chamber bowl. The room was highly insanitary with no ventilation, excrement and urine on the walls from a previous patient, and poorly lit. The applicant was always in bed clothes with no covering for his feet and he had virtually no opportunity for exercise or association.

The length of time in seclusion and the conditions were themselves worrying, although MIND had for some time known that his case was not atypical. What was of concern was the fact that the hospital justified the seclusion as 'treatment'. Yet isolation from one's fellows in the most primitive conditions could not, according to all the psychiatrists who gave evidence, be considered therapeutic. Further, since Broadmoor was simply not used to being persistently questioned on its justifications, it became clear that it misled the European Commission. In its first statement to the Commission it said that the patient was highly excited and agitated and was under medication for the purposes of bed rest. The hospital authorities were then asked to release the nursing notes which read 'patient calm and cooperative'. The medical notes showed that, contrary to what

69

the government told the commission, he was never under medication.

The case, brought under Article 3 of the European Convention of Human Rights which prohibits inhuman and degrading treatment, was settled. The terms of the settlement were an *ex gratia* payment of £500 and the adoption of minimum guidelines for the use of isolation. However, in representing the applicant the author then wrote to the commission on 13 March 1980:

We observe that Sir George Young, Minister for Health, in response to a Parliamentary Question (Wed., 16 Jan. 1980) said 'the main effect of the guidelines is to clarify previously unwritten practices rather than to introduce changes'. The acceptance of the substantive terms of friendly settlement should not be taken to imply that we accept that the guidelines are adequate to prevent a repetition of the circumstances which gave rise to a finding of admissability in respect of Article 3 of the European Convention on Human Rights.

The existing guidelines for seclusion in the special hospitals are a useful and constructive first step. But it should be noted that at present they have no statutory force. Moreover, the use of seclusion is not specifically regulated under the Mental Health Act 1983 or accompanying regulations. It is to be hoped that the Mental Health Act Commission will not only include new guidelines on seclusion in its code of practice but that seclusion will be added to the forms of treatment for which consent and/or a second opinion is required under section 57 or 58 of the 1983 Act.

The Martin case

The use of seclusion in the special hospitals continues to cause serious concern. Michael Dean Martin died in his cell at Broadmoor on 6 July 1984. From evidence given at the inquest by Broadmoor staff and patients, it appears that events leading to his death started with an argument between himself and another patient, who had been taunting him with racial abuse. Staff refused to intervene when asked to by Mr Martin, who then took a swipe at a nurse, but missed. According to a patient present in the room, a nurse then applied a 'vicious neck hold, pulling him to the floor'. He was overwhelmed by staff, taken to a side room and stripped. Several patients heard a 'short, strangled cry' followed by silence. Mr Martin had been injected with the maximum dose of sodium amytal (500 milligrammes) and 200 milligrammes of another tranquilliser, Sparine. These added to his routine daily medication of tarctan and Melleril meant he had received a total of 1100 milligrammes of medication.

The nurses should have checked whether Mr Martin had eaten before the injections. On a full stomach, the drugs can cause vomiting and, eventually, choking because of the failure of the body's gag reflex. Broadmoor's guidelines for secluded and sedated patients say that they must be observed every fifteen minutes. According to evidence, Mr Martin was visited only twice during his hour-and-a-half seclusion. On the second visit he was found dead. The immediate cause of death was given as 'aspiration of stomach contents', although the Home Office pathologist pointed out other factors: multiple bruising around the neck 'consistent with pressure from an arm or arms' and 'general signs of an episode of asphyxia' which may have been caused by pressure to the neck.

Evidence was given of routine and heavy medication of patients by nurses without advice from doctors. Nurses had not been trained to restrain aggressive patients without doing them serious harm (such training is now being given at Broadmoor and Rampton). The verdict was 'accidental death, aggravated by lack of care'. For further details of evidence at the inquest see the transcript, part of which is recounted in *Open Mind* (MIND 1985).

The independent public enquiry into Mr Martin's death, presided over by Shirley Ritchie QC, recommended the employment of more qualified nursing staff and occupational therapists in order to improve patients' quality of life and prevent the build-up of frustration in patients and staff. Nursing staff should be trained in the physical control and restraint of patients, the new course at Broadmoor to become a compulsory and regular part of nursing training at the hospital. Heavy sedatives should be administered by doctors only, at the time of the incident, with full knowledge of the extent of violence and the quality and quantity of food recently consumed by the patient. The observation of a heavily sedated patient should be constant and in the room in which he is confined.

Censorship

There is a reasonably strong case to suggest that today there is seldom, if ever, a need to read systematically the correspondence of mental patients. Yet there is a long and protracted history of this occurring. Broadmoor and Rampton hospitals both specifically employ 'censors' to read all incoming and outgoing correspondence. At Broadmoor correspondence is also often read by nurses and doctors, and we have always had the impression that letters to and from MIND's Legal Department were being read. In one case, after several patients had written to MIND asking for a representative before a tribunal, the consultant announced at a ward meeting that they would be detained longer if they applied to a tribunal since that would only detract from their treatment.

When representing Broadmoor patients before the European Commission and Court of Human Rights it came to my attention that all of the correspondence with my client was being read. These letters included detailed strategy for the commission and court hearings and it was clearly wrong for the other party to see them. MIND appealed to David Ennals, then Secretary of State for Social Services, who gave an unequivocal undertaking that the letters would no longer be read. Yet, medical staff intentionally disobeyed the orders of the Secretary of State and continued to read correspondence.

When the White Paper on the Mental Health Act was published (DHSS 1978) it proposed the removal of most of the powers of censorship and made no special arrangements for the special hospitals. But there was quite intense lobbying by the special hospital doctors and, as a result, the new Act provides little if any protection for patients. So weak are the new provisions that while, nominally, the decision on censorship is to be taken by the hospital managers (that is, the DHSS), section 134(7) says the managers' responsibilities 'shall [not 'may'] be discharged on their behalf by a person on the staff of the hospital'. Broadmoor has authorised all of its medical and nursing staff to do this and it is the only hospital which opens all correspondence from, and to, MIND. It is difficult to see how correspondence to MIND staff is 'likely to cause distress to the person to whom it is addressed', as section 134(1) requires before post can be withheld.

Control over the exercise of this kind of arbitrary power affecting the lives of patients can only be provided by the Mental Health Act Commission which hears ultimate appeals over decisions to withhold correspondence. The powers of the commission do not extend to section 134(4) which authorises the opening of post to see if anything in it must be withheld. Yet, the commission has taken a strong and principled stand in such cases of clear circumvention of the Act.

Complaints

MIND and NCCL receive numerous complaints from Broadmoor patients, ranging from minor incidents on the wards to ill-treatment and neglect. No doubt not all the complaints are true. Yet, it is crucial that they be thoroughly investigated by an independent authority. The Rampton Review Board found that of over 40 complaints made by patients not one was upheld. MIND had the same experience with the other special hospitals and made intense efforts to obtain the cooperation of the DHSS in getting some kind of rigour and independence in the investigation of complaints.

In one case a patient wrote to MIND alleging that he had been ill-treated by certain ward staff. He gave times, dates and reasons. MIND made a complaint to the Secretary of State as the manager of Broadmoor in the expectation it would not be dealt with internally. Several weeks later the reply came: 'This case has been investigated by nursing staff on [the ward in question] and they have not substantiated it.' A complaints procedure which is undertaken by fellow professionals will never inspire the confidence of the public or patients. But one which virtually asks those people against whom the complaint is made to carry out the investigation is totally unacceptable.

It is the responsibility of hospital managers to investigate complaints but unfortunately, despite the criticisms in the Boynton report (DHSS 1980a), the situation has deteriorated. As the Rampton Review Board (1983) said to the Secretary of State: 'With regard to complaints the board share the department's concern about the present procedure for dealing with allegations of ill-treatment, currently not capable of being investigated by the hospital management team'.

The reason for the absence of any complaints procedure by the hospital managers at *all* of the special hospitals is that the Prison Officers Association has passed a national resolution refusing to cooperate with any internal investigation. All cases of maltreatment must be referred to the police and cannot be investigated by the managers with the cooperation of the staff. The review board rightly 'regards this as not only a constraint on local management in that inadequate information is available about allegations of professional misconduct, but also as a practice which is not always in the best interests of staff'.

Police investigations of serious allegations of criminal offences are, of course, essential. But there are many cases where ill-treatment is not serious enough to warrant prosecution; there may be sufficient evidence to take disciplinary procedures, although not to obtain a conviction. Management and the nursing profession have a high responsibility to be sensitive to patients' complaints and to ensure that they are examined carefully. A complaint may be justified even though it is not substantial enough to warrant involvement by the police. For example, a criminal prosecution requires the police to meet a 50 per cent test that a jury will find the crime proved beyond a reasonable doubt. If sensible managers had to adopt that rigid a test every time the behaviour of a member of staff was giving cause for concern, they would be unable to take action. That is precisely the intention of the POA industrial action, and it has succeeded.

The absence of a fair and effective complaints procedure in the special hospitals is probably the most important illustration of the deep-seated attitudinal barriers that must be overcome.

Transfer and discharge

In recent years some two thirds of releases from special hospitals have been by way of transfer. This trend of transfers over discharges declined in 1984 (DHSS 1985). The total number of patients who left special hospitals in 1984 was higher than in the previous year – 285 as against 215; the number of discharges rose from 71 to 95; transfers to the Eastdale unit dropped from 12 to 10; and transfers to local NHS hospitals dropped considerably, from 132 to 102.

Despite the decline in transfers in 1984, the most likely route out of a special hospital is still by way of transfer, not discharge, and this is with good reason. Anyone who has spent a long period in a high security institution will require a time of relaxed security under care and supervision in a local hospital, allowing for a gradual return to freedom and normality. It is helpful to the patient because it allows him to adjust to increasing amounts of freedom while still receiving treatment, care and support; and it protects the public because the authorities are able to test how the patient is coping before he is discharged back into the community.

There has been persistent grave concern about the difficulty of transferring patients from the special hospitals. In an important report Suzanne Dell (1980) showed that there were 183 patients in the special hospitals who had been recommended for transfer but for whom no local hospital bed could be found. She suggested that many more might be suitable for transfer but were not being recommended because doctors were beginning to feel that recommendations had little chance of being implemented. Also, patients in hospitals where (as at Rampton) there was a high turnover among doctors were at a significant disadvantage so far as transfer was concerned. It takes time to get to know a patient well enough to form a view as to his suitability for transfer, and a constant change of doctors ensures that transfer recommendations will be infrequent. It is also clear that in some hospitals different doctors take very different views about suitability for release; a patient's chance of being recommended for transfer depends less on him than on his doctor.

The Dell report caused a storm of protest and the Secretary of State personally intervened by writing to every regional health authority to try to get them to accept their responsibilities towards patients (*The Guardian*, 12 November 1980). More recently the DHSS has held a number of meetings in NHS regions to discuss with those concerned locally the problems which can arise over the transfer of special hospital patients. Meetings have also been held with representatives of social services departments to discuss problems associated with the movement of patients out of special hospitals (Parliamentary debates 1984a). Early in 1985 the chairman of the Rampton Review Board wrote to regional health authorities who had a responsibility to provide beds for patients at Rampton who were awaiting transfer.

Despite the storm of public protest and the direct intervention of the DHSS, the problem has not subsided but has indeed increased since 1979. At that time there were 183 special hospital patients on the transfer list. At the end of 1984 the figure had risen to 233 despite a substantial fall in the special hospital population; this meant that some 12 per cent of the special hospital population were formally awaiting transfer. By far the greatest problem was at Rampton where 110 patients were waiting, of whom 59 per cent had been on the list for over a year. Of the total waiting list of 233 patients, 26 had been waiting for two to three years, 20 for three to four years, 7 for four to five years, 3 for five to six years, and 6 for more than six years. (Figures in the text were the position at 31 December 1984 (DHSS 1985), while figures in Table 2 were the position at 23 July 1984.)

Table 2* Special hospital patients awaiting transfer to NHS hospitals

	Total	Under 1 year	1–2 years	2–3 years	3–4 years	Over 4 years
Broadmoor	41	30	8	1	—	2
Moss Side	49	23	16	7	3	—
Park Lane	24	14	9	—	—	1
Rampton	112	46	27	15	11	13
Total	226	113	60	23	14	16

* Figures derived from Parliamentary Answer given by Mr John Patten, Under-Secretary of State for Health (Parliamentary debates 1984a). The information is the position as at July 1984. At that time there were also 12 special hospital patients awaiting transfer to the Eastdale unit at Balderton Hospital, Newark, with one patient having waited 1–2 years and another 2–3 years.

This is a national scandal because it means that there are mentally disordered men and women who are continuing to have their liberty infringed to a far greater extent than is necessary. Moreover, a patient who remains in a special hospital longer than he should loses hope and his condition deteriorates. The problem has been known for many years but it has been considered an 'administrative' difficulty: 'If only the NHS could be persuaded of their responsibility to admit patients who no longer require special security'. (See Chapter 1 for the reasons why local hospitals are reluctant to admit patients.)

The problem of transferring patients is not as great in other countries, particularly in North America and Europe. In the United States the constitution and courts will not allow a person to be detained in conditions unjustified by his dangerousness and his mental condition. In Europe, most hospitals cannot or will not refuse to admit patients recommended for transfer from high security institutions. It is suggested that sufficient opportunity has been given to allow informal, administrative solutions to the problem in this country and that Mental Health Review Tribunals should now be given the power to *direct* the transfer of special hospital patients. We have for too long regarded the opinions of professionals as more important than the rights of patients. What explanation can be given to a mentally handicapped patient at Rampton who has remained in an environment which totally restricts his freedom for more than four years after his doctor has said he no longer needs to be there? As the Rampton Review Board (1982) wrote: 'The efforts of psychiatrists and social workers are often thwarted by the unwillingness of NHS hospitals, hostels etc. to accept ex-Rampton patients ... The DHSS must ensure that patients who no longer require the secure environment offered here are transferred more quickly as there is evidence of deterioration in patients thus held back'. The Review Board expressed the same concern in its 1983 report.

Conditional discharge and after-care

There are also patients formally awaiting a conditional discharge from a special hospital for whom there is no home or hostel place to go to or whose after-care arrangements have held up the discharge. As at the end of 1983 there were 43 patients in this position (see Table 3). Again, note that virtually half were at Rampton. This meant that some 17 per cent of the special hospital population was either awaiting discharge or transfer; at Rampton and Moss Side it was 22–23 per cent.

Table 3* Special hospital patients awaiting conditional discharge

Date	Broadmoor	Rampton	Moss Side	Park Lane	totals
31 12 79	29	20	2	2	53
31 12 80	16	17	1	3	37
31 12 81	13	11	5	5	34
31 12 82	4	15	5	8	32
31 12 83	6	20	4	13	43

* Figures are taken from DHSS (1984) and represent the position at 31 December 1983.

Local authorities are often very reluctant to provide residential care and support for patients who have been in special hospitals. This is partly for the reason given by local hospitals – that patients may be disruptive or dangerous. But there is another problem, which concerns finance. So long as a patient remains in hospital the cost of his case is borne by the NHS. Consequently, local social services departments have an in-built motivation to try to maintain that a particular individual should be the responsibility of another agency (for example, another local authority or the NHS), for, by doing so, they avoid overloading already stretched facilities. In one case a special hospital patient had remained on the waiting list for some two years. He lived in the catchment area of the Kent County Council who refused to take responsibility for him because they claimed that, originally, he lived in the area of another local authority, which was also refusing responsibility. After a long period the two authorities agreed costs. Thereafter the staff in the residential home in Kent refused to take the patient, without even seeing him or his records. Caught in the middle was a patient who should have had his freedom in the community but remained in a special hospital instead.

There have been many attempts to solve the problem, including the operation of joint funding arrangements between health and local authorities, and placing the responsibility for after-care services on health and local authorities in section 117 of the Mental Health Act 1983. Support for special hospital patients after their discharge is crucial for their welfare and for the protection of the public. In many cases where serious crimes have occurred after a special hospital patient has been discharged, there was little or no follow-up support or supervision. The duties of the social services, the health services and the probation services sometimes overlap, and it is clear that boundaries between these services must be removed as a matter of urgency. (See McFarlane and Wells 1984: 'The fact that different facilities are provided from different budgets constantly bedevils the rational allocation of resources to the mentally disordered.') A recent example is the attempt by the Oxford Regional Health Authority to transfer the care of mentally ill people to the community. This has met with strong opposition from the local authority for which there are resource implications.

There are proposals by MIND (1983) for the setting up of a mental health service development committee in each area to develop strategy and policy; and a mental health service development group which would conduct the operational planning, budgeting, control and management of the new mental health service. MIND's initiative for a better coordinated local approach should be encouraged.

There is also the possibility of extending joint funding, and the active enforcement of the after-care provisions of the Mental Health Act, under which patients should be given the express right individually to enforce the after-care duty in a court of law. Finally, the Boynton report (DHSS 1980a) recommended extension of the existing arrangement whereby the DHSS can make extra-statutory payments to local authorities to maintain ex-special hospital patients in hostels. The Rampton Review Board (1982) noted that there has been little or no movement on this. The board felt that this proposal should go forward more quickly and be extended to the NHS. These are sensible proposals which should be implemented.

Structural problems of the special hospital system

In this section it is intended to examine the structural problems in the special hospital system and to suggest reforms. The problems in the special hospitals already identified should be seen as causally linked to a system which concentrates some 1,500 patients, selected for their supposed dangerous and criminal propensities, in four hospitals on only three sites. The special hospital system should not be viewed narrowly but be seen as an integral part of the entire network of secure provision for mentally disordered people in England and Wales. This being so, it is remarkable that the introduction of an entirely new level of secure provision, in the form of regional secure units (see Chapter 5), has brought about very little, if any, constructive planning as to how the special hospitals should fit into the network of secure provision.

Concentration of special hospital patients

Admission to a special hospital can mean that patients are moved many hundreds of miles from family, friends and past or prospective employers. This inflicts hardship on patients and their families, making contact very much more difficult and sometimes impossible. It also badly impedes the extent to which they can pursue rehabilitation, since few of these patients will be intending to live in the community close to the hospital. Thus, quite apart from the local community's attitudes, it is difficult practically to arrange much in the way of local employment in normal settings on day release, or to encourage regular home visiting.

Concentrating the special hospital population on only three sites has produced large institutions with insular and closed attitudes;

MIND referred to these as 'company towns' because the staff housing is on the hospital campus and there is a long tradition of having a close-knit staff community. The management of the hospitals – particularly Rampton and Broadmoor – must reckon with an ideology not merely subscribed to by people at work, but one which binds a community together. The community is well organised to defend its attitudes against threats to change the settled régime. There is every reason to expect that in this kind of setting staff transfers will be low. In Rampton, for example, many staff give their working lives to the hospital. While this dedication is to be admired, it brings with it the extremely serious problem that few outsiders committed to modern therapeutic and rehabilitative ideas find working at the special hospitals attractive. Even if they did it would be difficult to progress very far against the prevailing practices. Appointments to senior nursing posts are most often made from those well schooled in the ways of the hospital. Nursing staff in the special hospitals are the most cohesive group. They live together, work together, and share many of the custodial attitudes of a time gone by.

One recent illustration of the propensity to take a narrow view on matters of staffing was the decision to re-appoint a nurse who was *convicted* of ill-treating a patient at Rampton. It is very difficult to see how this decision can be justified. We expect the highest standards from staff in special hospitals; to re-appoint a person to the same hospital where he was convicted of mistreating patients must be regarded as insensitive management at best, and unprofessional at worst.

The hospital management team at Rampton has tried very hard to change these attitudes and to instil therapeutic principles. The service given, for example, by Dr Alf Minto, until recently the medical director, has encouraged a therapeutic ideal and provided a model for other doctors to follow. This has clearly assisted in solving the perennial problem of recruitment of high quality medical staff. Yet, the HMT has a long way to go before being able to claim any fundamental attitudinal change in the nursing staff. The shift system still exists in virtually the same form as when Boynton condemned it (see page 67); staff for some time refused to supervise day trips for patients (see page 63); and the POA have prevented the implementation of any effective complaints procedure (see page 73). The recent public statement by the chairman of the Rampton POA that genuine communication is 'nil' is only illustrative of the wide gulf between a new HMT committed to a therapeutic institution, and a staff still schooled in the ways of custody. The scenario, of course, is not as simple as this, and highly dedicated staff are to be found at Rampton and the other special hospitals. But it would be wrong not to weigh these factors very heavily in deciding future policy for secure provision for mentally disordered people.

Isolation from the rest of the NHS

For the reasons given it has been impossible to achieve the 'attitudinal swings' that the Boynton report thought necessary. The special hospital system will continue to carry unavoidable and inherent therapeutic costs so long as it is in the shape of large institutions divided from the rest of the mental health services by stark barriers of functions and management, and with insufficient cross fertilisation of people and ideas.

There is a clear need to establish better contact between people in the special hospitals and mental health professionals in the NHS. It is essential that doctors, nurses and other professionals in the special hospitals are exposed to the ideas, experiments, successes and failures of people outside the walls of the special hospitals. There should be staff exchanges – including in-service training outside the hospital – refresher courses and study visits built into the ordinary life of each special hospital. Low staff turnover should be seen as a warning that staff may be 'trapped' inside the special hospitals. Career structures in the NHS and the special hospitals must promote easy movement between the two systems. Staff housing policy may also need to be reassessed, and specific model programmes of good practice established within the hospitals, involving staff seconded from outside, to demonstrate different techniques and attitudes in action.

Truly multi-disciplinary teams should be involved in planning patients' resocialisation programmes, a process that should involve consultation with the patients' families and active encouragement of contact between them and the patients; the staff also should get to know the families and the patients' contacts in the community.

The most encouraging signs of change in the special hospitals have occurred in the foregoing areas. Through new management, the special hospitals have gradually come to see the desirability of shared training and appointments with the NHS and academic institutions. New joint appointments and training schemes have been developed at Rampton and Broadmoor, and this progress should be encouraged.

Openness

1 *The media*

Almost every report into the special hospitals has expressed concern at the closed and insular attitudes of staff. Neither of the major television documentaries on Rampton (Yorkshire TV) and Broadmoor (Central TV) received any cooperation from the hospitals and filming was not permitted on the premises. Perhaps this is unsurprising since much of the media has had a perverse concern with the background of patients, invading their privacy and causing unnecessary alarm among the public. But the way that patients are treated, the conditions of confinement, and the rights and dignity afforded to them *are* legitimate matters of public interest. It cannot be right that the media should have been given so little cooperation in relation to a public institution providing services under the NHS. Information about special hospitals must rightfully be within the public domain.

Some of the special hospitals have recently been seeing the advantages of allowing increased access to the media, subject of course to the wishes of their patients for privacy. Radio and television companies have been allowed into Park Lane, Moss Side and Rampton. This is a welcome development although a cautionary note must be added. The POA at Rampton have shown signs of resistance to the atmosphere of openness promoted by the Rampton Review Board and the HMT at the hospital. In 1983 a full contingent of press was invited by the medical director to see the hospital, but was turned away by the POA.

In 1984 Alison Hyde, from the *Health and Social Services Journal* was repeatedly blocked from entering the hospital. She was finally allowed in and wrote her account in the 29 November 1984 issue of the journal. Her conclusion: 'Maybe it is not beyond the realms of possibility that a radical re-think could take place. It does seem after a long campaign for a visit that Rampton needs revolution rather than evolution to bring about real change.'

2 *The Official Secrets Act*

Remarkably, all the staff in special hospitals are asked to sign the Official Secrets Act, and are required to seek permission for any statement made on the special hospitals, including professional articles. One can readily understand the necessity to keep security details secret, but the Act also covers any information about employment, including professional/clinical matters, conditions of confinement and the like. While the DHSS has made it easier to obtain permission for publication (through a senior staff member at the hospital) the fact that the Act continues to apply to all disclosures adds to the suspicion and distrust from the outside. Indeed, doctors at Park Lane were recently chastised by the DHSS for writing a letter to *The Guardian* about services in the NHS. They were also prevented from holding a professional conference at the hospital to discuss a draft copy of this King's Fund report.

3 *Advice and information agencies*

It is extremely important that special hospital patients, because of their vulnerable position, have access to people from outside the hospital to provide them with impartial advice, information and, where necessary, representation. At Park Lane the local community health council was given facilities inside the hospital so that it was in a better position to provide patients with advice. This development is an important example of good practice which other special hospitals could adopt. (Middleswood Hospital, Sheffield, and Tooting Bec Hospital, London, have similar arrangements with citizens advice bureaux.) Broadmoor had an approach from a CHC for this purpose but did not support the idea.

It is equally important that independent monitoring agencies have access to patients and the opportunity to speak to them in confidence; that these agencies actually take up this opportunity on a regular and ongoing basis; and that they do not feel that their position is so tenuous and weak that they are restrained from actively pursuing problems and complaints and, where necessary, bringing them to the attention of the appropriate officers or the public. In many cases these agencies may want to represent patients or ensure that they are represented by solicitors.

4 *Legal representation*

Legal representation is also important for special hospital patients, particularly at mental health review tribunals. Rampton has a long tradition of encouraging this and even maintains a list of local lawyers. Broadmoor, however, has been hostile to the concept for some time. A highly professional group of lawyers and voluntary organisations within the Oxford Regional Health Authority set up a scheme of representation for patients at MHRTs, but have failed to gain cooperation from Broadmoor. This is a narrow approach to patient care. Patients must be regarded as citizens with rights as well as needs. It is wrong to set the need for therapy against entitlement to safeguards and representation; they are not contradictory and both should be encouraged by staff in special hospitals.

Therapeutic community

It is a hallmark of life in the special hospitals that patients are given very little control over their own lives and in the running of the ward. A number of institutions abroad receiving patient groups comparable to the British special hospitals are dedicated to an active therapeutic community. The need to minimise the patient's perception of custody and to maximise his control over his own life is taken for granted. The Van Der Hoeven Clinic in Holland, for example, has a system of committees, on which patients sit, which decides many issues of management. Patients are looked after by staff of both sexes as a deliberate policy; they have private rooms; and the clinic is situated in Utrecht, a town with many facilities (like a swimming pool) which the clinic shares with the local community. It would be desirable for some of the British special hospitals to implement a similar therapeutic community principle. At the moment, a genuinely high standard of care does not exist in some of our special hospitals. A higher standard is more likely to be found in some of the regional secure units which are at least freshly and properly staffed, suitably located and reasonably small.

Management: the need for integration with the rest of the NHS

As was explained earlier, special hospital management, unlike the rest of the NHS, is centralised. There are currently two distinct levels of management in the special hospitals. The first is the internal management which is responsible for the day-to-day care and treatment of patients. This form of management, usually led by a medical director, has been unable to effect the kind of change necessary for the creation of a genuine therapeutic environment. It is a closed system of management. Even though the special hospitals are public institutions, professionals and the public outside the system have little idea of what goes on. The public would have greater confidence in an independent management structure which is composed of, or at least includes, individuals who are not members of the hospital staff. Thus the management team might include professionals from the NHS (solidifying links between the special hospitals and the rest of the Health Service) and lay members; it might indeed have a legal or lay chairman. An independent management structure would create a required form of check and balance and could monitor and effect change from the outside and without the handicaps inherent in self-examination.

A second line of management is through the Secretary of State, exercised by the DHSS. It is bound to be said that successive Secretaries of State have failed badly in their role as managers; MIND observed, for example, to the Rampton Review Board that the DHSS must either have known of the abuse or neglect of patients, or they should have known if they had been carrying out their management functions properly. As indicated earlier in this report it is likely that the DHSS had some idea of what was going on (although perhaps not to the full extent), but were simply unable to stamp their authority on the hospital.

The DHSS is too distant an organisation to manage special hospitals, some of which are hundreds of miles away from the department. Also, managing the special hospitals in a different way from the rest of the NHS causes isolation and separates the two systems. It is doubtful that any experienced observer could disagree with this assertion, and many who have looked into the matter have come up with similar conclusions (for example, see DHSS 1976a).

Local Management

It is therefore proposed that each of the special hospitals is managed by a health authority – either a regional, district or special health authority. The management of Rampton Hospital certainly has benefited from this kind of arrangement.

The Rampton Review Board is a special health authority which considers itself a non-executive management committee. They have undoubtedly made remarkable improvements in the hospital, in attitudes of staff, conditions of confinement and therapeutic programme. The benefits of local management are that it is near to the hospital and can observe its problems at first hand. Proximity means that the managers can see the patients, staff and facilities more frequently and work with the hospital management team and staff to effect change. Because they are appointed from outside the system the board can help introduce fresh ideas and a fresh and independent perspective. They should work from the outside to promote the rights, welfare and dignity of patients. There is a strong case for extending the Rampton experiment to the other special hospitals.

While the establishment of a special health authority to manage Rampton has resulted in substantial improvements, even further advantages could be gained by devolving management to existing regional or district health authorities and by introducing regional catchment areas. This could help bring special hospital patients closer to the communities to which they will return and reduce the formal separation and isolation of the special hospital system from the rest of the NHS. There are clear advantages, for example, in having common management of all hospitals in a region, with highly secure provision truly integrated with all other health services. The opportunities that a policy of dispersal of management would provide to resolve problems of isolation, size, tradition and fabric are highly appealing.

Reducing the size of special hospitals

It is clear that the special hospitals (especially Rampton and Moss Side) have many patients who ought not to be there, no matter which view is taken. Probably between a half and two thirds of the patient population could be discharged or transferred. This is derived from the figures already presented of those formally on the waiting lists to be transferred or discharged (see Tables 2 and 3); those who are civil patients or who have not committed serious offences; and mentally handicapped people, particularly severely mentally handicapped people, who should not be in a special hospital. (Dr Alf Minto, the former medical director at Rampton, has, for example, repeatedly made clear that less than one third of the hospital population actually needs to be there). In future, courts should, where appropriate, direct more psychopathic offenders to be sentenced to imprisonment where they can be cared for in a reformed Prison Medical Service (see Chapters 1 and 2).

The future

The problem for the future of the special hospitals is how a hospital of some 250 patients should be run. Many of the patients will not come from the region where the special hospital is located and should not be cared for there.

Given these numbers it is clear that Moss Side as a special hospital is untenable. There are simply too few patients to make its continuation necessary, and too many associated problems of staffing, security and treatment. If Moss Side is to remain in any form (and this should not be assumed automatically) it might serve as a regional secure unit or as a non-secure local hospital.

Rampton also should be much smaller and there is a strong case for closing the hospital in its present location (in an orderly, phased manner) and building new regional facilities close to centres of population, medical schools, universities and other hospitals.

The future of Broadmoor and Park Lane too must be considered carefully. Certainly Broadmoor must exist as a much smaller institution and Park Lane should not expand any further. The development of secure provision in the NHS should not continue to rely so heavily on maximum security institutions with national catchment areas, and outmoded facilities. Inappropriate staff attitudes also pose formidable obstacles to achieving a more humane and compassionate form of patient care. Almost everyone recognises that if we were to start afresh in developing secure services we would not devise Victorian and isolated institutions like Broadmoor and Rampton. We now have the opportunity to carefully examine our policies, with the introduction of regional secure units. The Secretary of State must seriously consider the long-term role of special hospitals. If high quality and compassionate care of patients were the primary considerations, it would be surprising if the special hospitals were maintained in their present form.

Summary of recommendations: The special hospitals

Most of the following recommendations presume that special hospitals will remain in one form or another, particularly because the DHSS has precluded any realistic shorter term proposals by embarking on a major rebuilding programme at Broadmoor and by the building of Park Lane, a new special hospital. But, in the longer term, it is proposed that the special hospitals should be phased out, first by transferring Moss Side to the regional health authority or district health authority as part of the secure provision in the region, or as a local hospital. At the same time there should be a continued and major contraction at Rampton and Broadmoor.

Informal patients should not reside in a special hospital

1 *Informal patients should not reside in the special hospitals because of the difficulties of obtaining meaningful consent, and because of the highly secure and closed conditions. If this proposal were to cause real hardship, for example to patients who lived most of their lives in a special hospital, the cases should automatically be reviewed by the Mental Health Act Commission.*

Non-dangerous patients should not reside in a special hospital

2 *Patients who are not of 'dangerous, violent or criminal propensities' should not be detained in a special hospital. A Mental Health Review Tribunal should have the power to direct the transfer of patients not meeting the statutory criterion.*

Children or young persons should not reside in a special hospital

3 *Only patients over the age of eighteen should be eligible for admission to a special hospital.*

Nursing

4 *Nurses in special hospitals should have their sole loyalty to, and identity with, psychiatric nursing, shown by their membership of a professional association or health service union, in their dress and in their training and experience.*

Improving conditions

5 *There is an urgent need to improve conditions and maintain more privacy for patients in the special hospitals, particularly Broadmoor and Rampton – for example, by improving sanitation, bathing and toilet facilities and making better arrangements and facilities for fire precaution. These changes have already begun in earnest and are to be welcomed.*

Rehabilitation

6 *More serious attention should be given to rehabilitation of special hospital patients by allowing them freedom in the hospital grounds (already done at Broadmoor, and planned at Rampton), making*

occupational therapy more widely available, offering them choice in the running of the ward, and by granting more frequent opportunities for trips outside the hospital and leaves of absence. The social services department should play a key role in devising an individual rehabilitation and resocialisation plan for each patient.

Treatment

7 *Every special hospital should have an ethical committee recruited predominantly from people outside the hospital and with a reasonable number of legal and lay members. The committee should consider not only research proposals but treatment issues affecting the interests of patients. The decisions of the ethical committee should be open to public scrutiny and be binding upon the hospital.*

8 *The use of seclusion and restraint should be carefully regulated in the code of practice which is being prepared by the Mental Health Act Commission; they should also be included under the Mental Health (Hospital, Guardianship and Consent and Treatment) Regulations 1983 so that consent and/or a second opinion would be required before they are imposed. New minimum guidelines for the use of seclusion should be introduced.*

Censorship

9 *The Mental Health Act 1983 should be amended to require the hospital managers to exercise more direct control over the opening of post in special hospitals. The Mental Health Act Commission must be congratulated for exercising close control over the opening of post in inappropriate circumstances.*

Complaints

10 *The hospital managers must devise a system of investigation of complaints which is independent, rigorous and involves the patient.*

11 *The Mental Health Act Commission, particularly until recommendation 10 is accepted and implemented, must ensure the proper investigation of complaints and, if not satisfied, must undertake the investigation itself. The Commission has shown itself to be diligent and effective in its work.*

Transfer, discharge and after-care

12 *Patients who are judged fit should be immediately transferred to an appropriate local NHS hospital. Mental Health Review Tribunals should have the power to make a binding direction for transfer.*

13 *MIND's proposals in* Common Concern *(MIND 1983) for a better coordinated local approach should be implemented.*

14 *Joint funding arrangements should be extended and funds specifically directed towards care of the mentally disordered offender in the community.*

15 *The Mental Health Act should be amended to give detained patients the right individually to enforce section 117 (the duty to provide aftercare) in a court of law.*

16 *There should be an extension of the present arrangement whereby the DHSS can make extra statutory payments to local authorities to support ex-special hospital patients in hostels and in other residential accommodation. This arrangement should also be extended to the NHS.*

Monitoring procedures

17 *At each of the four special hospitals there should be an independent monitoring body, such as a law centre or Citizens Advice Bureau. The independent agencies must have unimpeded access to patients and the regular opportunity to speak to them in confidence. These agencies must take up the opportunity to interview patients on a regular, systematic and ongoing basis; they must not be made to feel that their position is insecure and tenuous, or restricted in their pursuit of problems and complaints and, where necessary, bringing them to the attention of appropriate officials and the public.*

Exchanges between special hospitals, local hospitals, academic centres, the family and so on

18 *The special hospitals, local hospitals and academic centres should more actively seek cross-fertilisation of ideas and the exchange of people. Staff exchanges, including in-service training outside the hospital, refresher courses, study visits, joint appointments and so on should be built into the ordinary life of each special hospital. Progress in these areas should be encouraged.*

19 *Truly multi-disciplinary teams should develop an individual resocialisation plan for each patient in consultation with his family. The hospital should encourage active contact between the patient and his family, and the staff should get to know the family as well.*

Therapeutic community

20 *A special hospital like Broadmoor or Park Lane should seek to*

establish an experimental period to put into operation a therapeutic community of the kind operated at the Van der Hoeven Clinic in Holland.

Management: The need for integration with the rest of the NHS

21 *There are currently two forms of management structure: internal management running the special hospitals on a day to day basis, and the hospital managers (that is, the DHSS through its Office Committee of Special Hospitals) who carry out the functions given to them by the Mental Health Act 1983. The public would have greater confidence in the daily running of the special hospitals if they had an independent management structure including individuals who were not members of the hospital staff. Thus, the management team might include professionals from the NHS (solidifying links between the special hospitals and the rest of the health service) and lay members, and might have a legal or a lay chairman. The second tier of management should be delegated to regional, district or special health authorities who would more fully integrate the special hospital services with the NHS.*

The future

22 *The special hospital population should be reduced by one half to two thirds. The rest of the patients currently in the special hospitals should be discharged or transferred. This would include patients formally waiting to be discharged or transferred, civil patients and those who have not committed serious offences, and mentally handicapped (particularly severely mentally handicapped) patients. In future the courts should, where appropriate, divert more psychopathic offenders to a reformed Prison Medical Service (see Chapters 1 and 2).*

23 *This would mean closing Moss Side since it would not have a viable patient population. Its future (if there is one) would be reconsidered; it could become, for example, a regional secure unit or a non-secure local hospital for mentally handicapped people.*

24 *Rampton, Broadmoor and Park Lane should each be reduced to a population of some 250 patients. The question arises, in particular with Rampton, whether these three hospitals should close in their present locations (in an orderly and phased manner) and whether new regional facilities close to centres of population, medical schools, universities and other hospitals should be built. Rampton, much more than the*

other special hospitals, suffers from isolation and an unhealthy tradition. While the post-Boynton management has made great improvements, they have not been able to overcome many of the custodial traditions in the hospital. Most urgent consideration therefore should be given to Rampton.

CHAPTER FOUR

Local hospitals

Background: the 'open-door' policy

The Royal Commission (1957) and the Mental Health Act 1959 provided a symbolic turning away from the legal and custodial aspects of the old lunacy laws. Several policies very clearly emerged in the late 1950s and 1960s. Patients, whenever possible, would receive treatment on an informal basis; they would be treated in the same way as physically ill patients in open wards and, increasingly, in district general hospitals. The ultimate goal was to return the patient to the community. New and distinct terms arose in that era that are still put forward as enlightened concepts – the 'open-door' policy, the 'therapeutic community' and 'community care'. Not only was there new legislation in the form of the Mental Health Act 1959 which made this therapeutic revolution possible, there was the advent of the major tranquillisers which were to play a part in the unlocking of doors on previously closed wards.

The 'open-door' policy was undoubtedly correct since the great majority of patients should continue to enjoy their freedom while receiving treatment in a local mental illness or mental handicap hospital. Treatment under open conditions affords the patient a degree of liberty and dignity which cannot be achieved if the doors are locked. The therapeutic effects of open conditions are also evident. Patients must be constructively occupied on the wards; occupation and recreation must be provided outside the wards; the patient must be respected as a person and treated with patience and gentleness; there must be good communication between staff and patients; and the constant aim on the ward must be resocialisation of the patient (Faulk 1985). Studies showed also that patients should receive material benefits, such as improved clothing, holiday visits and private posessions, and the staff should be continually stimulated and supported (for example, Stern 1957).

The conclusions reached by many mental health professionals from the studies of open wards and their own clinical experience was that the restrictions produced by locking doors had a marked adverse effect on the relationships between patients and staff, and the degrading experience of being confined had caused anxiety and additional mental health problems. As a result there has been a pronounced move away from the use of closed wards in local hospitals.

There is considerable evidence that staff in local hospitals have, indeed, lost much of their will and capacity to care for and treat difficult or disruptive patients. Courts have sometimes had to sentence mentally disordered offenders to prison, and prisons have been unable to transfer many seriously mentally disordered offenders to the NHS (see Chapters 1 and 2). Special hospital patients who do not require a high degree of security have been unable to find a bed in the NHS and potentially difficult or dangerous people in the community have been unable to obtain care in the NHS. Thus the movement away from the use of closed wards in local hospitals has had a telling impact on the whole of the mental health service. If local hospitals do not take a full share of responsibility for difficult or disruptive mentally disordered persons the strain will be felt in the prison medical service, the special hospitals, regional secure units and the community. In short, the difficult mentally disordered person, once cared for in locked wards in the hospitals, has lost his place in the NHS and is today to be found in prisons, special hospitals, borstals and on the streets – often passing from one institution of social control to another.

As early as 1961, a Ministry of Health report warned of the dangers of dispensing with security precautions in local hospitals. Hospitals which did not have well considered security plans made applications for transfer to special hospitals more often than others. Sometimes hospitals even exaggerated the behaviour of their patients to convince the DHSS of the need for a transfer. Once admitted to a special hospital, a patient has little chance of being taken back into the NHS for a lengthy period; indeed the patient will carry a record of exaggerated behaviour with him indefinitely, making any progress back to the community more difficult. It has also been shown that the likelihood of a hospital taking difficult mentally disordered people is greater if the hospital has a locked ward (Bowden 1975).

Scope of the problem

There is very little evidence quantifying the need for secure provision in local hospitals. A study by Oxford University (1976), of the number of people in the Oxford region who might require security within the NHS showed substantial unmet need. A study in

Camberwell (Wykes, Creer and Sturt 1982) showed a need for security for 13 per 100,000 population, or some 6,500 per 50 million.

Given the fact that the courts and parts of the mental health service have experienced great difficulties in finding beds in local hospitals for difficult patients, and the empirical evidence described above, it appears that local hospitals are not providing an adequate service for those mentally disordered people who require care under some conditions of supervision and control, but are not sufficiently dangerous to be placed in prisons, special hospitals or regional secure units. The Glancy report (DHSS 1974) confirmed this by suggesting that there were 13,000 patients in local hospitals who required some degree of security, and whom the hospitals wished to transfer to more secure hospitals. But the security provided by the hospitals was neither planned nor therapeutic, simply involving locking doors, the use of seclusion and physical restraint. Often doors have been locked in wholly inappropriate cases – for example, elderly wandering patients and severely mentally handicapped patients.

Where hospitals have maintained locked wards they have often not been part of a well considered security plan, but have been caused by staff shortages; it is cheaper and administratively convenient simply to lock a door to contain potentially wandering or disruptive patients than to increase the number of staff. The fact that this is professionally unsound is obvious, but it is also unlawful. It is, for example, false imprisonment to lock the door on an elderly wandering patient, usually in hospital on an informal basis. So too is it unlawful to use seclusion or physical restraint unless there is an urgent need to prevent danger to the patient and other people (see Chapter 7).

Current policy

The problem of inadequate security in local hospitals has been widely accepted by successive governments. So too has the solution – the development of regional secure units, which is dealt with in Chapter 5. Here it can be said that the units provide an overly simplistic administrative response to the complex problem posed by the reluctance of local hospitals to work with difficult cases.

If regional secure units are to have a place in a well planned provision of secure services for mentally disordered patients it is clear that their role will have to be restricted to the more dangerous patients who require confinement for a period of twelve to eighteen months. Usually they will be offenders or people who, if they escaped, might be immediately dangerous.

Virtually no attention has been given to the much more significant problem of non-offending difficult or disturbed patients and the way local hospitals are to cope with them. Regional secure units are intended only to deal with a small proportion of potentially dangerous patients unsuitable for special hospitals (Bluglass 1978). Some provision will have to be found for difficult patients elsewhere. If the problem of where to place difficult patients is not addressed carefully, and solutions found, the same pattern of neglect of this group will continue to the end of this decade and beyond. In the remainder of this chapter an attempt will be made to address the problem of how local hospitals can become a truly integral part of the mental health security services. Indeed, it is suggested that local hospitals should play the central role in the provision of secure services.

The trend towards highly specialised maximum and medium secure hospitals is certain to erect barriers between the various parts of the health service. It makes it more difficult, not less, to have an easy flow between the levels of secure services, and exacerbates the problem instead of resolving it by enabling patients to progress steadily to lesser forms of security and restraint and eventually back into the community. By creating establishments labelled 'secure', we also label the patients in them, and make it more difficult for the patients to be accepted for treatment in local hospitals near their homes. Patients are seldom either dangerous or not dangerous; rather, they are dangerous only at certain times and in certain situations (Bowden 1985). It therefore makes little sense to admit the majority of difficult patients to a secure unit where they are continuously under a relatively high degree of control and restraint. The more sensible placement would be a local hospital with open conditions but with the resources to provide an extra degree of supervision and control when it is required. Once the need for security has passed it is administratively very simple to return the patient to an open environment. The patient benefits by being in a hospital close to his family which does not label him as permanently dangerous with all the accompanying stigma. Also, there are no formidable administrative barriers attached to a transfer from a more to a less secure hospital.

Closed wards can produce therapeutic environments

Although it has often been assumed that closed wards have inherent therapeutic costs, if the proper therapeutic environment is provided the locking of a ward need not necessarily have harmful effects (Folkard 1960; Cobb and Gossop 1976). These studies show that the benefits in a hospital ward depend primarily on therapeutic activity, not on whether the doors are locked. Further, it is the positive interaction between patients and staff, as opposed to the facilities for restraint, which reduces patient aggression (see the interesting analysis by Faulk 1985).

It is essential that the NHS plans carefully for local hospitals to develop a capacity to provide treatment and care for difficult patients. The question is what staffing, resources and training will be needed to enable local hospitals to provide the very best treatment and care for an entire range of mentally ill and mentally handicapped patients, excluding only those who would be immediately dangerous if they escaped.

Special care unit

Local hospitals should consider the feasibility of establishing a 'special care unit' for the more difficult patient. With a higher staff–patient ratio than other parts of the hospital, the unit would provide a greater degree of supervision and control and would be strongly therapeutically oriented. The unit would assist the hospital in caring for patients when they become violent by taking them in until their behaviour returned to normal; this might be hours, days or weeks. It would reduce the number of patients sent to regional secure units and absorb acutely disturbed people (from admission wards, for example, or the chronically ill suffering 'flare ups') under the best conditions to enable a swift return to 'open' wards. Similar wards have been recommended by COHSE (1977) and have been tried successfully on an experimental basis (Woodside and others 1976; Carney and Nolan 1978).

In essence these 'special care units' are very similar to the better interim secure units (Faulk 1979a). The South East Thames Regional Health Authority (1979) has developed a model of good practice. It is planning a central regional secure unit with four smaller secure clinics in other parts of the region. The concept to be emulated is to attach a small special care unit to a hospital so that there is no formal administrative difference between residence in the hospital and in the unit, enabling an easy flow between the two.

Resources, professional guidance and training

It will not be simple or inexpensive to ensure that local hospitals have the capacity to provide quality services with a reasonable degree of security. A substantial level of resources is needed to provide more staff and better facilities. There is also a strong need for better staff training, particularly nurses, to help them to cope with potentially dangerous patients. It is not surprising that many nurses have negative attitudes towards closed wards. They are usually understaffed, overcrowded, dirty and degrading for staff and patients alike. Nurses are left without reasonable support or professional guidance, and have no training; as a result their morale suffers. They are even being subjected to an alarming number of assaults (COHSE 1977) and it is small wonder that the union has had local bans for nearly ten years on the admission of mentally disordered offenders. Although it is totally wrong for nurses to take industrial action affecting patients in this way (a mentally disordered person may be sent to prison if no local hospital bed can be found) the sentiments of a regional chairman of COHSE can be understood, nevertheless.

> We are not trying to undermine the authority of the courts, but we are thinking of our members. What is being suggested is that these men be put on a ward where at night there may only be one member of staff on duty who is untrained and a slip of a seven stone girl at that.

In an effort to provide guidance, the DHSS published a circular on the management of potentially violent patients in 1976 without consulting COHSE, which represents most of the psychiatric nurses. COHSE (1977) felt the guidance was wholly inadequate, and rejected it.

Nurses, by the nature of their profession, take primary responsibility for the day-to-day care of patients. They remain with patients in sheltered environments for long periods, often without the full support and understanding of management. It is essential that they are given professional guidance and training to deal with potentially violent patients. More important, they need staffing and resources on a much larger scale than at present to enable them to do their jobs properly. It is beyond the terms of this report to give such professional guidance; the author does not have the expertise to do so (COHSE 1977). But there is also a strong need for guidance and training on the law. At the moment mental health professionals have very little idea about their powers and duties in restraining and treating detained and informal patients. Some basic guidance is provided in Chapter 7 (see also Hoggett 1985; Gostin 1985).

Conclusion

The difference between 'special care units' and regional secure units is a matter of degree only. But careful consideration needs to be given to how they are to co-exist in a fully integrated mental health service. It is clear that both should be attached to local mental illness or mental handicap hospitals, or to district general hospitals. The role of special care units is to provide an intense therapeutic environment with unobtrusive supervision and control, and to be therapeutically oriented they must be adequately resourced with sufficient well trained staff. Their existence would help to prevent many patients being sent to regional secure units or to special hospitals. Regional secure units would remain small and could achieve their primary objective of relieving congestion in the prison medical service and in special hospitals. Patients, wherever possible, would be cared for without suffering the stigma of a specialist secure hospital; they would be nearer their homes, their families and prospective employers. Given the proper resourcing to achieve a high quality of care combined with a degree of security, patients can be looked after in a humane, therapeutic environment. The trend towards a total 'open-door' system in special hospitals, while understandable and born of good intentions, has robbed the mental health service of its capacity to deal locally with its most difficult patients. It is time for the pendulum to move gently in the other direction and to introduce well planned and well resourced secure services in local hospitals as part of a fully integrated mental health service.

Summary of recommendations: Local hospitals

Special care units

1 *Special care units should be established in local hospitals, providing a high degree of supervision and control in a highly therapeutic environment.*

a) *There should be no administrative differences between the unit and the rest of the hospital, allowing for an easy flow in and out of the unit.*

b) *A patient should receive greater supervision and control only for the period in which he is immediately dangerous; ordinarily, admission to a special care unit would be for hours, days or weeks.*

Resources, professional guidance and training

2 *A substantial level of resources should be provided to local hospitals to enable them, in a planned way, to develop the capability of dealing with potentially difficult or disruptive patients. Nurses and other mental health professionals urgently need:*

a) *Professional guidance on the management of potentially dangerous patients. This could be provided, for example, by a working party specially established and comprising the DHSS, the relevant Royal Colleges (for example, Nursing and Psychiatry), the relevant health service unions, and voluntary organisations.*

b) *Training in the management of potentially dangerous patients. The working party could make recommendations for training. In the interim, voluntary organisations, such as the King's Fund, MIND or MENCAP could provide a valuable training service.*

c) *Professional guidance and training in the law relating to treatment and restraint of mentally disordered persons. Mental health professionals, particularly nurses, must be aware of their powers and duties in dealing on a daily basis with informal and detained patients (see Chapter 7).*

Integrated service

3 *Secure services in local hospitals must be well planned in order to fit in with other secure services in the region (see Chapter 6). The difference between regional secure units and special care units should be one of degree only. Both should be attached to local hospitals or district general hospitals. Special care units would look after people who, if they absconded, would not be an immediate danger. Thus most patients could be cared for locally, and local hospitals would not have to transfer so many patients to regional secure units or special hospitals. Regional secure units could then better achieve their primary objective of relieving congestion in the prison medical service and in special hospitals.*

CHAPTER FIVE

Regional secure units

Background

There was no lack of anticipation or warning about the effect of the 'open-door' policy in local NHS hospitals. The Royal Commission (1957) proposed that dangerous patients should be accommodated in a few hospitals having suitable facilities for their treatment and custody. The idea was then taken up by the Ministry of Health in a circular to the regional hospital boards, hospital management committees and boards of governors in May 1959, two months before the Mental Health Bill received the Royal Assent. The Ministry, warning against indiscriminate application of the 'open-door' principle, advised that there were 'some patients – not all of whom may have been before the courts – for whom the maintenance of adequate security precautions must be regarded as an essential part of their hospital care, either for their own interest or that of the community'. Two methods of achieving this security were outlined: the first was for each hospital to maintain some special security precautions; the second was the establishment of special secure units within each regional hospital board.

In July 1959 the Minister of Health, Enoch Powell, appointed a working party to consider the provision of security in psychiatric hospitals and the future task of the special hospitals. The working party report (Ministry of Health 1961a) welcomed the 'open-door' movement but concluded that some hospitals should continue to provide a variety of units of different types, including some designated secure units, so that transfer between them could be made without difficulty according to the patient's needs. The working party suggested that before a person was admitted to a special hospital, he should be considered for admission to a regional secure unit so that his needs could be assessed: 'Admission to a special hospital should be arranged only when it seems clear that there is no other course open.'

The Ministry of Health issued a circular to regional hospital boards in July 1961, advising them how to implement the working party's recommendation – but not a single secure unit materialised. One reason for this may have been the lack of money.

The idea of regional secure units was reintroduced in 1974 in the interim report of the Committee on Mentally Abnormal Offenders chaired by Lord Butler (Home Office 1974). The committee was 'astonished and shocked' at the overcrowding in special hospitals and pointed to the increasing number of mentally disordered persons in prison. It proposed 'as a matter of urgency' the provision of secure units in each regional health authority. It was estimated that 2,000 beds would be needed. The committee urged the government to finance the units by allocating funds directly from central government.

The revised report of the Working Party on Security in NHS Psychiatric Hospitals chaired by Dr Jim Glancy (DHSS 1974) was published at about the same time as the interim Butler report. It also recommended the development of regional secure units, but proposed 1,000 instead of 2,000.

On 18 July 1974 the Secretary of State for Social Services, Barbara Castle, said in Parliament:

I accept the recommendation of both reports [Butler and Glancy] that urgent action should be taken to establish in each health region, secure psychiatric units ... We shall begin by providing a total of 1,000 places and if the need is confirmed by experience, will build up, as and when resources permit, to the 2,000 places recommended by the Committee on Mentally Abnormal Offenders.

The DHSS issued a circular of guidance to regional health authorities, agreeing to make a direct grant to the regions for the establishment of secure units (DHSS 1974a). The government's financial undertaking at this stage was limited to providing the capital cost of the units. The initial response was highly equivocal. In its final report (Home Office 1975), the Butler committee stated its concern that little progress had been made in establishing the units, or even in providing temporary arrangements for 'interim secure units' as the committee and the government had urged. The committee recognised the difficulty in finding sufficient suitable staff, but noted that financial recognition (a 'lead payment') for nurses who would work in the units had been negotiated. But many regional health authorities had not even submitted plans for the units, and it was considered that their obligation to meet future running costs from revenue might be a discouragement. Consequently it was recommended that running costs should also be met from central government funds.

There was a swift response from the government and in January 1976 it announced the establishment of a special revenue allocation to be provided annually until secure units were fully established. It was to be given to regional health authorities according to their populations and was based on the initial need of 20 beds per million people. The money was used to support interim secure units and was intended to be approximately two thirds of the estimated revenue required.

The DHSS said it expected a 'substantial number' of the 14 regional health authorities to begin work on the construction of units (by adaptation or new building) in 1975/76, and that all regions should have begun construction by 1976/77. Yet during that period, although 10 of the 14 regions had made some interim arrangements, only Yorkshire, South Western and North Western authorities had started to building their units.

Nineteen years after the DHSS first decided that there was an urgent need for regional secure provision, England's first and, until 1983, only regional secure unit providing thirty of the originally planned sixty beds opened in the grounds of St Luke's Hospital, Middlesbrough.

The revenue allocations for secure units have been diverted to other services

The commitment to establishing regional secure units was so low that much of the money that was given directly by central government for the revenue costs of secure provision was not spent; it was simply absorbed into other 'higher priorities' in the health regions. Often the money was spent on general health care provision and was not used for the mental health services at all.

From 1976/77, when the central revenue support was first made available, to 1981/82 (latest national figures available) £44,285,000 was allocated to regional health authorities for the provision of secure facilities in the mental health services. Yet the proportion spent on secure facilities was only seven per cent of that sum in 1976; it had risen to forty per cent by 1981/82 (see Table 4). Thus, during this period, over £26 million directly allocated for secure provision for mentally ill and mentally handicapped patients was not spent for that purpose. More than £12 million was spent on general medical services having nothing to do with mental health. In 1982/83 a

Table 4 Total revenue allocation received by regional health authorities with amounts spent on security in psychiatric hospitals and on other psychiatric services. In £000s

Regional health authority	Total revenue allocation 1976–77 to 1981–82	Expenditure on security in psychiatric hospitals 1976–77 to 1981–82	Expenditure on other psychiatric services 1976–77 to 1981–82
Northern	2,956	2,158	—
Yorkshire	3,389	2,178	251
Trent	4,340	553	2,773
East Anglia	1,719	425	1,093
North West Thames	3,283	1,001	1,082
North East Thames	3,533	261	2,570
South East Thames	3,432	1,706	199
South West Thames	2,761	2,003	338
Wessex	2,523	1,618	—
Oxford	2,093	561	845
South Western	2,998	552	758
West Midlands	4,957	1,725	2,379
Mersey	2,388	1,246	771
North Western	3,913	1,915	1,224
Totals	44,285	17,902	14,283

Source: Parliamentary debate (1982b).

further £10,800,000 was allocated centrally for secure provision but no spending figures are available (Parliamentary Debates 1982b).

The Oxford Regional Health Authority has a particularly disappointing record and today still has no plans for a regional secure unit for mentally ill people. Between 1976/77 and 1979/80, £1,168,000 was allocated to the authority for secure provision, but *none* of it was spent for that purpose. From 1976/77 to 1983/84 more than £3 million was allocated, but only just over £1 million spent on secure provision in psychiatric hospitals. Plans for secure provision for mentally handicapped people at Borocourt Hospital, Reading, have now been approved. Since 1976, funds for capital expenditure have been available from central government for the building or adapting of units for secure provision, yet the Oxford RHA has claimed none (Parliamentary debates 1984a).

It is worth considering for a moment why there has been so much resistance to the regional secure unit programme, even though central government funds were available. An analysis may provide an insight into the problems inherent in the concept of regional secure provision. The major problem is attitudinal, both in the NHS and among the general public. Secure provision is thought to be concerned with a relatively small group of patients for whom there is often little sympathy and minimal understanding, but who appear to have attracted preferential financial support when other patients considered to be more deserving are feeling the effects of economic restraint (Bluglass 1985).

Another important reason for the delays has been the reluctance of local communities to accept the presence of secure units. This is an inevitable result in a community of any proposal to site a unit which provides accommodation for 'special' individuals. Patients are presumed to be immediately dangerous if they escape. The community therefore resists the project and, if it proceeds, erects attitudinal and physical barriers to any meaningful association of patients with the neighbourhood. Indeed, the early experiences of regional secure units indicate that professionals and members of the public were already prejudging the patients. For example, South West Thames proposed to build a secure unit immediately beside the Royal Earlswood Hospital. Local residents drew up a petition of protest. COHSE described it as a 'dastardly scheme'. Mr George Gardiner, the local MP, called it a 'monstrous injustice'. The newspapers referred to the proposed unit as a 'mini-Broadmoor' (*Daily Telegraph*,

23 April 1976). Mr Gardiner summed up the feelings of the community: 'No site proposed for such a security unit, designed to accommodate criminal elements, will ever be greeted with enthusiasm by local residents.'

Mr James Callaghan MP (Middleton, Prestwich) said the secure unit planned at Prestwich Hospital has caused 'great alarm, anxiety and fear ... The public needs assuring that the doors, windows and fencing of the security unit will give maximum security'. In September 1976 the secure unit at Rainhill Hospital, St Helens, was supposed to open, but NUPE refused to staff it because of the danger to staff and local residents. They wanted a 17 foot high perimeter fence.

In the end several regions had to submit to non-statutory public planning enquiries (for example, South Western region) and occasionally a local pressure group successfully forced an authority to abandon initial plans and seek a site elsewhere (for example, SW Thames region).

Segregation and isolation

Many of these initial problems have now been overcome (see below), but they are worth recounting because they go right to the core of the problem of secure units and will persistently cause difficulties with staff and patients.

The fact is that they are separate, specially designed units with the exclusive purpose of caring for potentially difficult or dangerous patients. Every patient, past or present, is presumed to have dangerous or troublesome qualities. Indeed, the same patients who are regarded as socially acceptable while integrated in a local hospital attain an aura of dangerousness when they are resident in a 'special' or segregated unit. A major difficulty with any unit which is specifically set aside for certain kinds of patient is that all resident patients become tainted with the unit's image. This makes it difficult to prove, perhaps throughout the patients' lives, that they do not have the personal characteristics which are attributed to patients in those establishments. Far from helping patients to re-adjust and to become accepted again among their families and friends, they have the opposite effect. Those who plan the mental health services must come to realise that it is not simply the treatment and conditions in a hospital which are important, but the perception that other people in the NHS and the community have about it. As a general principle the more 'special' or 'segregated' the unit, the more difficult it is ultimately to gain the cooperation of the health and social services to facilitate the transfer and discharge of patients to less restrictive conditions. The unit also makes it more difficult for patients to become socially acceptable members of the community with a good chance of making friends, having a family, getting a job and finding a home. This principle has been termed by MIND as the right to the 'least segregated environment', which means that a patient should receive care and treatment in the least separate environment consistent with his needs.

The Confederation of Health Service Employees (COHSE) recognised this problem. It said the name 'regional secure unit' will have 'a profound effect on the image portrayed to the public at large', and it strongly recommended the title 'NHS Secure Treatment Units'. There is some merit in this suggestion, but the central problem is not the name of the units but their concept. Most units are relatively large, purpose built and quite separate from the general mental health services in the hospital to which they may, or may not, be attached (Snowden 1983). They therefore congregate people together from throughout the region and all are designated as security risks. If the units were to be a small integral part of a local or district general hospital, they would require no special name; they would not signal to the outside world and the rest of the NHS that their patients have special and undesirable personal characteristics.

The underlying aim, then, of a comprehensive mental health service should be to ensure that its clients who require secure provision should not, as far as possible, be segregated from other clients (MIND 1983). In practical terms this leads to some clear choices when examining the regional secure unit programme. Three kinds of provision have been proposed and developed: i) large secure units which are purpose built and take patients from the entire region; ii) smaller units (like the early interim units) closely associated with the local hospital to which they are attached and with the ability to exchange patients and staff easily between the unit and the hospital; and iii) a capability for secure provision in each psychiatric hospital. The first, the large separate secure unit, is destined to have difficulties because it is modelled closely on the special hospitals (albeit with a regional rather than national catchment area), and will suffer many of the problems of being separate and isolated from the rest of the NHS. Under current plans, approved by the DHSS, the largest units are to be in the West Midlands region (100 beds at Rubery Hospital, Birmingham) and North West region (88 beds at Prestwich Hospital, Manchester). The Trent region has a complement of 60 beds in Leicester, and Mersey region has a complement of 50 beds at Rainhill Hospital, St Helens (Parliamentary debates 1984).

The other types of unit fit in well with concepts of integration and fluid security proposed in this report. They would have the best chance of attaining an integrated range of secure provision consistent with local needs and resources. Indeed research has shown that the special care unit in a local hospital can be highly beneficial without the major disadvantages of segregation from the health and social services (see Chapter 4). Further, the interim secure units which very much fit into the second model (smaller units attached to local hospitals) have also been shown to be highly effective (Treasaden 1985). Thus eight years of experience with interim secure units and a new recognition of the importance of integrating secure provision into the mainstream of the NHS has led to a growing number of professionals supporting smaller units. Small domestic units of 15–25 beds are regarded as the most successful models (Higgins 1981; Faulk 1979; Bluglass 1985).

It is important to plan carefully by looking to the future and asking how patients, the public and mental health professionals regard a large purpose built unit? If the public fears its inhabitants, the professionals regard the patients as undesirable and unwanted, and the patients feel a sense of despair and loss of hope, what benefit will be achieved? And if the units become so segregated and separate from the mainstream of the NHS that patients are difficult to transfer or discharge, will it be necessary in several decades time to build different establishments to relieve overcrowding in the regional secure units?

The current position

All regional health authorities are now providing secure facilities of one kind or another. Six regions now have permanent regional secure units in operation (see Table 5; for regional secure units currently planned, see Table 6). The number of beds currently staffed and available in these units is 106. In addition, seven regions currently provide 260 beds in 13 designated interim secure units (see Table 7). The figures are as of July 1984.

Table 5 Number of beds in permanent regional secure units

Region	Location	Bed complement	Number of beds currently staffed and available	Date of opening
Northern	St Luke's Hospital, Middlesbrough	30	25	November 1980
Trent	Towers Hospital, Leicester	60	15	July 1983
East Anglian	St Andrew's Hospital, Norwich	36	10	May 1984
NE Thames	Runwell Hospital, near Southend	10	10	April 1983
South Western	Langdon Hospital, Dawlish, near Exeter	30	10	June 1983
Mersey	Rainhill Hospital, Prescot, St Helens	50	36	August 1983
		216	106	

Source: Bluglass (1985), updated by information given through direct personal communication with the DHSS.

In addition to the places provided in permanent and interim secure units, regional health authorities showed on their RSU returns in September 1983 about 900 further beds in other types of secure facilities in NHS hospitals – including special care and lockable wards. Regional health authorities regarded these beds as contributing to their regional secure provision.

All regional health authorities have now submitted plans for at least one permanent regional secure unit which has been approved by the DHSS. Regions' current firm plans include about 500 places in permanent regional secure units, all of which should be provided by the end of 1986 (see Table 6). By that time a number of other units are likely to be at various stages of construction and planning.

The Glancy report (DHSS 1974) envisaged a total of 1,000 beds in regional secure units, while the Butler report (Home Office 1975) recommended 2,000 beds (see above). The government's view is that it will aim for 1,000 but as the programme develops plans can be

Table 6 Regional secure provision currently planned

Region	Location	Beds	Progress
NW Thames	St Bernard's Hospital, Ealing	40	Tenders under consideration.
	2 further units also under consideration	30	Building expected to start in 1984.
SE Thames	Multi-site scheme:		Under construction; all units due for completion towards the end of 1984 or early 1985.
	Assessment unit, Bethlem Hospital	30	
	Area Unit – Cane Hill Hospital, Coulsdon	15	
	Bexley Hospital, Bexley	15	
	Oakwood Hospital, Maidstone	15	
	Hellingly Hospital, Hailsham	15	
SW Thames	Netherne Hospital, Coulsdon	25	
Oxford	Borocourt Hospital, Reading (mental handicap)	20	RHA reassessing policy for mentally ill (no RSU yet planned) in the light of their strategic shift towards community based services.
North Western	Prestwich Hospital, nr Manchester	20	Adolescent beds opening 1984.
		88	Adult beds, under construction, opening end 1984, early 1985.
West Midlands	Rubery Hospital, Birmingham	100	Building to start late 1984, early 1985.
Wessex	Knowle Hospital, Fareham	31	Conversion started October 1983. Due for completion soon.
Yorkshire	Fieldhead Hospital, Wakefield (mental handicap) completed November 1983	48	First patients to be admitted imminently.

Sources: Parliamentary debates (1984); Bluglass (1985).

110

changed upwards or downwards by actual demand on the places available in the interim and permanent units opened, and by evidence of research studies (Parliamentary debates 1983 and 1984a).

Table 7 Number of beds in interim regional secure units

Region	Location	Bed complement
Yorkshire	Stanley Royal Hospital, Wakefield	18
NW Thames	Leavesden Hospital, near Watford	62
SE Thames	St Bernard's Hospital, Ealing	14
	Oakwood Hospital, Maidstone	6
	Cane Hill Hospital, Coulsdon	6
	Bethlem Royal Hospital, Beckenham	15
Wessex	Knowle Hospital, Fareham	14
South Western	St Lawrence's Hospital, Bodmin	28
West Midlands	Coleshill Hall, Birmingham	8
	Lea Castle, near Kidderminster	18
	Barnsley Hall, Bromsgrove	12
	Central Hospital, near Warwick	15
North Western	Prestwich Hospital, near Manchester	44
		260

An example of good practice

The current stage of development in each of the regional health authorities is set out in Tables 5 and 6. For a full description, region by region, see Snowden (1983) and Bluglass (1985). Of particular interest are the plans of the South East Thames region which were set out in a publication by the authority in June 1979. The region has developed a unique model; a 30 bed unit attached to the Bethlem Royal Hospital, Beckenham, which has close connections with the teaching and research interests at the Institute of Psychiatry. This is to be used for assessment and has a region-wide catchment area. There are also four 15 bed area secure units at Bexley, Cane Hill, Hellingly and Oakwood Hospitals, each with a sub-regional catchment population. Patients transferred from special hospitals will be

111

able to go by planned stages of diminishing levels of supervision back into the community. The units are seen as part of the region's total mental health service, closely integrated with community services, and including sheltered work, social service support, probation and after-care support and medical and nursing care in the patient's own home.

The design of the units: problems and suggestions

Location and size

The Butler and Glancy reports emphasised that regional secure units should be placed in population centres, close to other medical facilities. It was envisaged that the sites would be in the local or district general hospital complex. The recommended size was 50–100 beds if the units could share facilities with the hospital, and 200 beds if they could not. It is now quite clear that regional secure units cannot become part of an integrated mental health service unless they are on local hospital sites, fully sharing facilities and with an easy exchange of patients and staff. Some planned units are so large and separate that there can be little or no interchange. Even the staff are unit-bound with the danger that they will become professionally isolated and inward-looking, running what is more appropriately called a secure unit service (Snowden 1983). A more ideal unit is the kind to be introduced in SE Thames where they form part of a more general mental health service. The staff work not only in the RSU but in the hospital and the community; they see outpatients and work for the courts and prisons. Some regions have displaced the RSU as the only service base. Both Mersey and SW Thames will have community bases for patient follow-up, teaching and research. It is clear also from what has been said in this report that a smaller unit of some 15–25 beds is recommended. It should be part of the local hospital and with sub-regional catchment area.

Patients

The White Paper on mental illness (DHSS 1975) made one of the few positive statements about the kind of patient who should be admitted to a regional secure unit: 'patients who are continuously behaviourally disturbed or who are persistently violent or considered a danger to the public, *albeit* not an immediate one.' The units are to admit most types of patient: offenders and non-offenders, formal and informal, male and female, in-patients, out-patients and patients

112

being assessed for the courts, adults and adolescents, and so forth. They are not intended for severely mentally handicapped patients who should be provided for in ordinary mental handicap hospitals.

It will be noted from Table 6, however, that both the Oxford and Yorkshire regions plan regional secure units for mentally handicapped people. Severely mentally handicapped people really should not be placed in regional secure units. They are seldom, if ever, determined absconders or seriously dangerous; and placing them in a unit makes the primary tasks of habilitation (that is, helping the mentally handicapped person to develop social and other needed skills) and education extremely difficult. It is sad to observe that there has been virtually no planning for mentally handicapped people who have been placed in secure provision, such as special hospitals. The regional secure units were developed to relieve over-crowding in special hospitals where by far the greatest problem is the need to transfer mentally handicapped people. Yet rightly, most regional secure units will not admit mentally handicapped people. There has also been no real planning of resources devoted to helping local mental handicap hospitals in caring for patients who need intensive care, support and supervision (see further Chapter 7).

Staffing

The DHSS (1975) strongly encouraged the adoption of a multi-disciplinary approach in secure units. This is very important, because the skills necessary for the treatment and resocialisation of mentally disordered people who require a degree of security include psychiatric nursing, social work, psychology and occupational ther-apy. The use of both men and women as staff is also highly rec-ommended because it reduces tension and creates a warm therapeutic environment, more closely reflecting social life in the community.

The recommended staff ratio of one nurse to one patient is likely to be 1:4.5. A high staff–patient ratio is vital to the success of a secure unit. It is always difficult to reconcile security and treatment; the more one is emphasised, the more the other suffers. The best way is to provide security through the constant supervision of staff, leading to a better relationship between staff and patient; and by the 'specialling' of particularly difficult patients (that is, assigning one or more staff to watch over and supervise a particular patient and to be sensitive to danger signs in his behaviour). Thus a high staff ratio can provide security which is as effective as the more obtrusive locked doors, bars and fencing, but without the therapeutic costs. It is clearly also important that staff should be given support and guidance in the management of potentially difficult patients, and receive sufficient training. Part of the training programme should involve a constant interchange with other staff in the NHS to gain experience of different ways of approaching professional tasks.

In order to attract high quality nursing staff a pay lead is given. This is likely to help recruitment, although Table 5 suggests that there has been difficulty in recruiting sufficient high quality staff for the few wards now in operation. One danger for the future is that the regional health authorities will not give the forensic service sufficient priority to keep the units running with the full complement of high quality staff. So far, all the interim units have maintained high staffing levels (Treasaden 1985; Reid and others 1982; Gudjonsson and MacKeith 1983). The danger is that in order to save running costs in future, regional health authorities will cut staff and the units will have to use more obvious forms of security, such as seclusion, physical restraint and locked doors. Indeed, there is an overall shortage of high quality nurses trained in caring for difficult or potentially violent patients. It has certainly been argued that regional secure units – because of the lead payment and the nicer conditions of work – will attract badly needed staff away from special hospitals and local hospitals, making their services even more inferior (Scott 1975).

Security

Regional secure units are not intended to provide as high a degree of security as special hospitals. They are not meant to try to contain a determined absconder or to prevent a rescue attempt. 'The units will be expected to stop patients simply walking out or otherwise leaving on impulse without staff knowledge' (DHSS 1975a).

Regional secure units should adopt a sophisticated and positive use of security. Non-physical aspects of security depend upon the skills and attitudes of the staff. Careful observation of patients and effective channels of communication serve to prevent dangerous situations. Patients should be given intensive psychotherapy and a great deal of individual attention to assist in trying to reduce feelings of tension and frustration. It is important to avoid undue restriction which breeds its own reaction. It is also important to detect and deal with worrying behaviour at the start. A unit should not require a perimeter wall, although perimeter security might be needed around a particular section for especially dangerous patients. There should be different levels of security in the unit, and every effort should be made to apply only sufficient security for the particular case. This is very important since there are clear dangers of falling into a routine use of too much security. Already there is a wide range of security measures in operation (or planned) at different units. Some adopt exceptionally obtrusive security, like barred windows and a high perimeter wall, which give the unit the air of a special hospital; on the other hand, some tend to use staff observation and an intensive therapeutic atmosphere to keep patients active and satisfied. Experience suggests that with good staffing and an active treatment programme the obvious forms of security can be kept to a minimum (Faulk 1979; Higgins 1979). Indeed, the Lyndhurst Unit at Knowle Hospital was run with perfect safety as an 'open ward' with most patients on controlled parole. Now it has two secure rooms and is locked at night, but only when required to be so during the day.

It is important that secure units provide the *least restricted environment* for treating the patient. The concept of *fluid security* is that each patient who is deemed to require some level of security during treatment should be subjected only to that level of security appropriate to his needs and only for as long as he requires it. This means in practice that all secure units should have a variety of internal security arrangements, and that the patient should ordinarily have the right to relatively free movement in the grounds unless he is likely to act dangerously. It is especially important that there is a pre-discharge section where the patient is free to pursue an active programme of resocialisation. If the unit is fully integrated with the hospital to which it is attached, patients from the unit should be free to walk in the hospital grounds and attend treatment, occupational therapy and recreation with other patients.

Length of stay

Secure units should aim to keep patients for as short a time as possible, and to have a high turnover of patients. If no progress with a patient is made after 12–18 months, an alternative placement should be considered (DHSS 1974). Regional secure units should not be afraid to take risks in an attempt to give their patients an opportunity to progress to a less restrictive alternative. The Lyndhurst Unit at Knowle Hospital, Fareham, has been able to

115

discharge patients quite quickly, but at the cost of a higher read-mission rate than the other interim units. It is suggested that this is justified because patients have developed a strong sense of hope and good relationships with staff.

The central question for regional secure units is whether they will be able readily to transfer their patients to local hospitals and discharge them into the community. If this is not achieved they will end up with patients remaining for many years and probably deteriorating, as is the case in the special hospitals. Early evidence from the interim units shows that this is not a problem for most patients, but that some are remaining for two to three years or more (Treasaden 1985). In many respects this is encouraging, for the units are not expected to find a less restrictive alternative in every case within eighteen months. This experience may well prove to be atypical, however. Most of them are small integrated units and it is reasonable to expect that their relationship with the NHS would be intact. The difficulty will come with the large segregated units. It is difficult to see any meaningful difference between regional secure units and the special hospitals, and it would be surprising if the units did not encounter the problems that have occurred at special hospitals.

Source of admissions

The regional secure unit programme will superimpose on the health service structure a new tier of secure provision at a great cost. There is little doubt that the 'haste bordering on panic' with which the government accepted the recommendations in the Glancy (DHSS 1974) and interim Butler reports (Home Office 1974) was based upon the urgent need to provide relief for the prisons and special hospitals. A major issue, therefore, is whether the regional secure units will achieve this objective. In 1977, MIND in *A Human Condition* (Gostin 1977) was concerned that much of the regional secure unit population could, if administrators were not careful, be drawn from the local hospital population. The Glancy report (DHSS 1974) pointed out that in 1971 some 13,000 patients (7.6 per cent of all those in psychiatric hospitals) were in wards that were locked during the day. This group included many who should not have been in secure wards – the elderly wanderer, the severely mentally handicapped and the patient who is only difficult during an acute phase of illness. There were also a significant number of patients in large wards who were kept locked up for the sake of a small proportion of difficult patients. In some hospitals, wards were closed as a compensation for serious staff shortages. Another factor was that of custodial attitudes – a reluctance to adopt open and active treatment methods. The Glancy report, on the basis of a survey of local hospitals, said that 1,258 patients in all were considered candidates for regional secure units.

Other more recent evidence suggests a substantial unmet need for secure provision in local hospitals and in the community (Sturt, Wykes and Creer 1982). Given that few new resources, guidance, training or encouragement have been offered to local hospitals to meet this need, the temptation to seek admission to secure units must be great. Whenever a highly specialised establishment like a regional secure unit is set up it is likely that people providing general mental health services will seek to transfer difficult patients to the specialised establishment. In this way, the creation of a secure facility to deal with disturbed behaviour may, if care is not taken, reduce the tolerance of disturbed behaviour in local hospitals. One particular manifestation might be an increased reluctance to accept patients direct from the special hospitals. It is probably true that demand for beds in secure units will increase with the number of places available.

These statistics bode ill for the regional secure unit programme, since there appear to be plenty of 'troublesome' patients in local hospitals to fill the 1,000 beds planned in the units. Indeed, when seeking to allay the fears of MPs concerned about the building of regional secure units, the then Secretary of State, David Ennals, said 'the patients for whom regional secure units are intended are mainly accommodated in the wards of ordinary NHS mental illness and handicap hospitals.'

The early evidence on the source of admissions to regional secure units fails to resolve this important question one way or the other. Studies of the operation of interim secure units show that over one third of all first admissions were from local hospitals. The remainder came from special hospitals, the courts, remand centres and prisons. It is arguable that this is too large a percentage to come from local hospitals since the main intention of the units was to take patients who were being subjected to greater restrictions on their liberty than in the units. Interim units, which are small and progressive, may not be a reliable indication of trend for the permanent units, particularly the larger ones. Clearly much more research is required, especially on the source of admissions.

Protection of the patient

The placement of any patient in secure conditions, particularly if he has not been convicted of an offence, is a serious matter and he has a right not to be there if it is unnecessary. Moreover, the question of whether a patient is dangerous is not easily answered (Bowden 1985), so that the decision about transfer to, or detention in, a secure unit, should not be a matter only for the professionals. A patient should be able to question decisions that would cause him to be detained in a more restrictive institution. He should be given all the reasons for the decisions and have the opportunity to present evidence contradicting them. Accordingly, Mental Health Review Tribunals should have the power to *direct* the transfer of patients to a less restrictive setting.

The likelihood of severe deprivation of liberty in a secure unit is why hospital staff should provide a statement of the patient's specific behavioural problems which require treatment under conditions of security; a description of the treatment goals, with a timetable for their attainment; the criteria for transfer to a less restrictive setting and when it can take place.

Conclusion

It is to be regretted that the government chose to embark on an expensive programme placing an entirely new tier on the mental health services. A unit which specialises in the treatment of potentially dangerous individuals separates itself and its patients from the mainstream of the health and social services. Therefore, the task is to make regional secure units as much as possible a part of the NHS. To achieve this, the ideal secure unit should be small (15–20 beds) with a sub-regional catchment area. It would be part of the local hospital to which it is attached and have a relatively free exchange of facilities, staff and patients with the hospital. It would have a high ratio of qualified and trained staff who would continue their education and training by exchanges with other parts of the NHS, the prison medical service, the probation service, the social services and academic centres.

Security would rely primarily upon staff observing, supporting and, above all, communicating with patients to forestall potentially dangerous situations. By using the concept of fluid security a patient would be subject to control, restraint or supervision only as a final resort, and only for the period of time strictly necessary. This would recognise that patients are seldom dangerous all the time. A good secure unit would carefully monitor dangerous circumstances to prevent them occurring, and provide, whenever possible, open conditions based on an active therapeutic philosophy.

Summary of recommendations: Regional secure units

Capital and revenue allocations for secure provision

1 *Any capital or revenue allocations from central government funds given for secure mental health provision must be spent for that purpose.*

Least segregative environment

2 *Patients have the right to the 'least segregative environment'. Thus, regional secure units should not be highly specialised establishments, set apart from the rest of the health and social services, but must be an integral part of a comprehensive mental health service.*
   a) *RSUs should be* **small**, *around 15–25 patients.*
   b) *RSUs should have a* **sub-regional catchment area** *so that they take patients who have family, friends and other contacts in the local community.*
   c) *RSUs should, for administrative and for virtually all other purposes, be* **part of the local hospital** *to which they are attached.*
   d) *RSUs should have a* **fluid exchange of patients** *and staff with the rest of the NHS, and particularly with the local hospital to which they are attached.*
   e) *RSUs must be seen to be an integral part of the region's total mental health services, closely integrated with community services, including sheltered work, social service support, probation and after care support, and medical and nursing care in the patient's own home.*
   f) *RSUs must have staff who receive training and do placements outside the units; there should be a full and continuing exchange of people and ideas. The staff must not become 'unit-bound' and every attempt must be made to make them 'outward-looking'.*
   g) *RSUs must have opportunities for full exchange with academic centres for training, education and research purposes.*

Least restrictive environment

3 *RSUs must provide the least restrictive conditions necessary to meet the needs of patients.*

a) *Wherever possible open conditions should prevail, as at the Lyndhurst Unit, Knowle Hospital, Fareham.*
b) *Security arrangements where needed should be unobtrusive. Sophisticated and constructive security arrangements include:*
   i) *a high staffing ratio which concentrates on careful observation and effective communication to forestall any potentially dangerous situations;*
   ii) *humane and warm staff–patient relationships to reduce feelings of tension or frustration;*
   iii) *the use of male and female staff which reduces tension and creates a warm therapeutic environment, more closely reflecting social situations in the community;*
   iv) *avoidance of undue restriction that breeds its own reaction;*
   v) *recruitment of well qualified staff to provide a high level of professional support, guidance and training on a continuing basis.*

Fluid security

4 *Patients should be under the minimum level of security required to meet their needs, and for no longer than is necessary. As soon as it is feasible, patients should be returned to more open and less restrictive conditions. In practice this means that all secure units should have a range of internal security arrangements:*
   a) *open conditions should usually prevail, including the right to relatively free movement around the hospital grounds and frequent visits to the community, for example, to family and friends and for shopping;*
   b) *there should be a pre-discharge section where the patient is free to pursue an active programme of resocialisation;*
   c) *the unit should be fully integrated with the hospital, and patients should be free to mix with patients from outside the unit, free to walk in the hospital grounds and to attend treatment, occupational therapy and recreation with other patients.*

Location, size and staffing

5 *The units should be in population centres and close to other medical facilities. In particular, they should be small and attached to local hospitals with which they would share facilities.*
6 *The units should adopt a truly multi-disciplinary approach in all their activities and decisions.*

Mentally handicapped patients

7 *The units should not be designed to admit severely mentally handicapped people. Comprehensive planning of secure provision for mentally handicapped people in local hospitals, social services accommodation and other community settings is urgently needed. A major problem in special hospitals is the hundreds of mentally handicapped patients who could be transferred if they had a better place to go to. Clearly RSUs are not intended for them. Careful thought has not been given to the rights and needs of this group of patients who remain without hope in maximum security conditions which they do not require. As a matter of urgency, the DHSS should set up a working party for mentally handicapped people similar to the Glancy committee. If the DHSS fails to respond, voluntary organisations such as the Independent Development Council for People with Mental Handicap should set up their own working party (see Chapter 7).*

Resources

8 *Central government and regional health authorities must continue to give a very high priority to financial resources for secure provision for mentally ill and mentally handicapped people. If revenue allocations are not maintained (and indeed, increased) in objective terms the units and local hospitals will not be able to appoint and keep high grade staff. Experience has shown that staff shortages and low staff morale cause more intrusive forms of security, including sometimes the unnecessary locking of doors and use of restraint and seclusion.*

Length of stay

9 *Patients should have the right to remain in secure conditions for no longer than is absolutely necessary.*
   a) *No one should enter a secure unit except as a last resort.*
   b) *The overwhelming majority of admissions to RSUs should be from the courts, the prisons and special hospitals, so that patients go from more to less secure conditions.*
   c) *Patients should leave secure units as soon as they are fit to do so.*
   d) *No one should remain in a secure unit for longer than 12–18 months.*
   e) *A patient should have the right to a Mental Health Review Tribunal which should have the power to* **direct** *his transfer when he is shown not to be in need of the conditions of security in the unit.*

Individual plan of treatment

10 *RSUs should provide a statement of the patient's specific behavioural problems which require treatment under conditions of maximum security; a description of the treatment goals, with a timetable for their attainment; the behavioural criteria for transfer to a less restrictive setting, and when it can take place.*

CHAPTER SIX

A coordinated approach for secure mental health services

The problems concerning secure provision described in this report are not new, and they remain unsolved. They are manifested in the courts' frequent inability to find NHS beds for seriously mentally ill or mentally handicapped people and, consequently, having to sentence them to imprisonment; in prisons being unable to provide treatment or humane care for mentally disordered people and being unable to transfer them to the NHS; and in a series of critical reports showing that special hospitals are separate and isolated from the NHS, and that a substantial number of their patients could be transferred if places in local hospitals were available. There are also research reports showing a substantial level of unmet need for security in local hospitals and in the community (Oxford University 1976, 1978; Wykes and others 1982). In short, there has been very little recognition of the needs of mentally disordered people who require some degree of security and, ever since the 'open-door' policy was introduced in the 1950s, the burden has increasingly fallen upon the penal system and the special hospitals.

As an answer to these problems successive governments have proposed an expensive, rather simplistic solution – regional secure units. There has been no comprehensive planning for the provision of security throughout the mental health services, and careful consideration has not been given to the way regional secure units would fit into a fully integrated mental health service. It has been thought that placing a new tier inside the mental health system would redress the difficulties experienced in each of the other levels.

Clearly the managerial and structural problems of each tier of the mental health services need to be examined. There is a substantial need for a comprehensive policy for secure provision throughout the mental health services. This would require a coordinated approach and would involve careful planning at national, regional, sub-regional, district, hospital and community levels; moreover, it would involve planning how each level could be linked with the others to provide a complementary and mutually supportive comprehensive service, with variable degrees of security.

Even if some of the more important recommendations in this report were implemented, the future mental health services for potentially difficult or dangerous patients would be changed substantially.

Sentencing and the penal system

The number of mentally ill and mentally handicapped people in prisons should be considerably reduced. This could be achieved by a shift in sentencing policy towards psychiatric probation orders, guardianship orders and other non-custodial 'therapeutic' alternatives; by the introduction and frequent use of remands to hospital for report and for treatment and interim hospital orders under the Mental Health Act, substantially reducing the number of unsentenced mentally disordered people in the prison system; and by making it easier to transfer mentally disordered prisoners to the NHS. Nevertheless, a considerable number of prisoners with emotional or psychological disturbance would remain for whom treatment and care would have to be provided. It will be impossible to make the Prison Medical Service an integral part of the health and social services while it is managed by the Home Office. The PMS would be in a far better position to help mentally disturbed prisoners if it were rooted within the NHS. Doctors, nurses and social workers would have far easier access to the prison and the transfer of mentally disordered prisoners would be greatly facilitated.

National or central provision of secure services

If special hospitals are to exist at all, they should be in an extremely reduced form. It is estimated that their population could be reduced by a half to two thirds by transferring patients to less secure hospitals. Special hospitals should not detain mentally handicapped people. If this were to happen at Rampton and Moss Side their populations would be so reduced that they could be phased out as special hospitals. It is also suggested that the management of special hospitals should be delegated to regional, special or district health authorities in order to give them the distinct advantage of being firmly rooted in the administrative structure which provides care and support to everyone else.

Regional provision of secure services

There are considerable doubts whether large secure units with 50–

100 beds and a region-wide catchment area are a satisfactory solution. There is no reason to believe that they would overcome the problems of isolation and segregation from the NHS which have plagued special hospitals for so many years. More epidemiological studies are required to show the extent of the need for secure provision; but at the moment it is doubtful whether there is a demonstrable need for both the continuation of special hospitals (albeit in the vastly reduced form suggested above) *and* large regional secure units. To ensure good staffing and ample resources, there may be a case for a region-wide secure unit for assessment purposes. But it would be of no benefit without sub-regional secure provision to ensure quick and trouble-free transfer of its patients.

Sub-regional (including several districts) secure provision

This level of secure provision has been absent for many years in the NHS, although it is now the model being used by the smaller, more innovative, interim secure units. These units have a more local catchment area, ensuring that patients remain near their families and friends, and allowing true integration with a full range of after-care and community services (see below). They are also integrated, managerially and operationally, with the local hospitals to which they are attached. This allows a wide exchange of staff, resources, therapy and patients. Unit patients are able to use the hospital grounds, helping in their resocialisation and avoiding the stigma of a separate and segregated 'secure unit'. Sub-regional units must continue to have an important and established place in the existing psychiatric services of a sub-region. They play an important localised role and form a key link in a chain of facilities providing varying degrees of security.

District and hospital-based secure provision

The future mental health services envisaged in this report would be capable of providing a certain degree of fluid security at every level. The district services and local hospitals would have the trained staff and facilities to cope with patients who were occasionally difficult and disturbed (COHSE 1979). This is absolutely essential in order to avoid the tension caused by local hospitals wishing to be rid of their problem patients, seeking to transfer them to more specialised units. Whenever possible, patients should be cared for in non-specialist environments with different sorts of people.

Community and after-care services

'Care in the community' has been one of the great unfulfilled prom-
ises of this generation, yet in the future pattern of services, particularly for patients who have been in secure psychiatric provision, it
will play a vital role. It is absolutely crucial that the after-care
provision in section 117 of the Mental Health Act 1983 should be
fully enforced. Under that provision, district health authorities and
local social services authorities, in cooperation with relevant voluntary agencies, must provide after-care services for any patient detained for treatment or under a hospital order. This after-care duty is
extended to cover all patients in need under para 2(1) of schedule 8
to the National Health Service Act 1977 which states: 'A local social
services authority may, with the Secretary of State's approval, and,
to such extent as he may direct, shall make arrangements for the
purpose of the prevention of illness and for the care of persons
suffering from illness and for the after-care of persons who have been
so suffering'. 'Illness' is deemed to include mental disorder within
the meaning of the Mental Health Act 1983. DHSS circular LAC
(74)19 *directs* local authorities to provide 'centres (including training
centres and day centres) or other facilities (including domiciliary
facilities) for training or occupation of persons suffering from or who
have been suffering from mental disorder' (DHSS 1974b). By virtue
of section 22(1) of the 1977 Act a local authority acting under powers
contained in schedule 8 is required to cooperate with the health
authority 'in order to advance the health and welfare of the people of
England and Wales'. (As to the local authority's duties to provide
services for mentally disordered people, see Gostin 1985.)

In a comprehensive mental health service, help must be given to
mentally disordered people in the community by the district health
authority (community psychiatric treatment and nursing), the local
authority (housing, education and social services support), and the
probation service (support and supervision for certain mentally disordered offenders). Strong links and channels of communication
must be established between these authorities and with those who
have been providing in-patient care (see below).

In particular the provision of services must not be seen as a matter
of charitable discretion, with the provision of a service by one
authority or the other depending upon a range of administrative and
financial factors. Instead, a patient should have the right to in-

dividual services (Gostin 1983a). The basis upon which a person should have access to services should be his need for those services, and everyone should have the right to equal care, concern and respect. The views, preoccupations and aspirations of the client or patient must be the primary force in the direction and development of services. It follows that a patient should have the right to be able to enforce in a court of law the provision of services to meet all reasonable needs. The Secretary of State for Social Services already has the power to hold health or social services authorities in default if they fail to carry out their obligations. Remarkably, the Secretary of State has *never* exercised his default power to promote the provision of mental health services. Much more constructive use must be made in future of the default power. In the last resort, the courts must be prepared to enforce statutory duties. Advocates for mentally disordered people must also be willing and able to bring appropriate cases to the attention of the courts.

A coordinated approach: the NHS

The real question for the future of the mental health services is how all the various levels of security can be integrated, and a planned coordinated approach adopted. It will be seen from the earlier description of services that one of the major problems which has plagued the mental health services is their inflexibility and the extreme difficulty they have in transferring patients to a different level of secure provision. Indeed, the way in which hospitals are responsible for specific catchment areas means that a patient refused admission by his own hospital will be denied entry to other hospitals, even those in the same district or region. What should be a national or regional health service is more like a feudal system, with each sector team reigning over its own strip. It is a sad reflection on the NHS (but no exaggeration) to say that often the final decision as to whether or not a special hospital patient or mentally disordered person is transferred depends entirely on *one* consultant who exercises total control over a catchment area bed. This is especially so where a hospital operates a strict geographical sector approach, targeting particular patients to a particular ward, or wards.

Central, regional and local hospitals, and community services, are kept apart by such stark barriers as separate management, competing financial interests, and different customs and attitudes. These barriers must be removed and new links formed between the different levels of service. At the moment, each level has separate managements which are, frankly, seldom coordinated or even knowledgeable about, or sympathetic to, each other's problems. Responsibility for the management of the mental health services is divided between the Home Office (Prison Medical Service and the Probation Service), the DHSS (special hospitals), regional and district health authorities (regional secure units and local hospitals), and local authorities (social services).

There is also a financial disincentive to accepting a transfer. As long as a patient stays at his level he remains someone else's financial problem. If a special hospital patient cannot be moved, the DHSS continues to pay for his care; if a patient is forced to stay in a regional secure unit, central government and the regional health authority will continue to share the cost of his care; and if a local hospital patient cannot find social services accommodation and care in the community, the district health authority, rather than the local authority, will have to bear the financial strain. Given their isolation and separation, and today's extremely tight budgets, it is not surprising that authorities are unhelpful towards each other. Staff and trade unions in some local hospitals and community facilities operate an absolute ban (varying according to category) on the admission of mentally disordered patients, restricted patients, or special hospital patients. Inevitably it is the patient who is the loser.

There need to be much fuller exchanges among the different hospitals of staff, patients and resources. Giving staff the opportunity to visit, train and work in other fields would expose them to new ideas and experiments, and to the successes and failures of staff outside the walls of their own institutions and environments. There should also be exchanges of people and ideas with universities and other academic centres, and joint cooperation in research endeavours. In sum there must be closer cooperation, more flexibility and easier movement among the various levels of institutional and community care.

To achieve the major objective of a fully coordinated and comprehensive mental health service in which barriers between the various levels are removed, it is important to uphold *the right to the least segregated environment*. In recent decades the NHS has taken increasingly a more 'specialist' approach to secure provision, with most of the difficult cases being sent to prisons and special hospitals. While this continues, there is little incentive for local and district general hospitals to genuinely seek a capability to care for the more difficult patients. Added to this is the fact that special hospitals and the Prison Medical Service have been isolated from the NHS, both managerially and professionally (see above). The outcome has been the segregation of difficult patients, unwanted by the NHS, in large centralised institutions. Arranging for these patients to enter local hospitals for care, treatment and rehabilitation has become painstaking, time-consuming and sometimes impossible. Patients remain in places like special hospitals for many years after they have been found fit to leave by a formidable consensus of responsible opinion – the medical officer concerned, the DHSS (the hospital manager), the Home Secretary (giving the necessary consent for a restricted patient) and a Mental Health Review Tribunal. They wait in maximum security conditions, often in despair, and with their mental condition deteriorating. The fact that they are in high security institutions makes it difficult for them to gain acceptance in NHS hospitals or in the community. They are treated as dangerous because of where they are, and without reference to their personal characteristics and past behaviour.

Is it the proper policy to have such large isolated institutions, separate from the mainstream of the NHS, designated to take only 'dangerous patients'? It is often uncertain whether or not the majority of patients are dangerous. 'Dangerousness' is an extremely complex concept, and professionals, including psychiatrists, cannot reliably say who will and who will not be dangerous (Bowden 1985). Usually, doctors tend to over-predict dangerousness. That is, they are far more likely to label someone as dangerous who will not be, than the reverse. The fact is that most patients are neither 'dangerous' or 'safe'; rather, they *may* be dangerous in certain situations and at certain times. In most cases, therefore, it makes very little sense to confine them in special institutions, or to keep them in a local hospital which lacks the capability to restrain them when the need arises. Any all-or-nothing decision is likely to be wrong. A patient confined all the time when he does not need to be is being needlessly deprived of his personal liberty, and the health service is spending money which could be used elsewhere. On the other hand, kept in the open conditions of a local hospital without trained staff and resources to deal with difficult behaviour, he may harm someone (either a patient or a member of staff).

The best solution to this dilemma is to introduce the concept of *fluid security* – the capability of restraining a difficult patient when necessary and of returning him to an open setting when he settles down. The degree of restraint should be the minimum necessary to ensure the patient's safety and that of staff and other patients.

This can be achieved by setting aside areas of the hospital where a higher level of supervision and control can be exercised. Obtrusive security measures are usually unnecessary. Instead, staff in sufficient numbers should be trained to detect and forestall potentially violent situations. Of prime importance are careful observation, a warm sympathetic therapeutic atmosphere, and a good relationship, with constant communication, between patients and staff.

A coordinated approach: health and community services

It is sometimes forgotten that the ultimate objective of care in the NHS is to return the patient to the community better able to cope with life. It is therefore essential that community support services form an integral part of a comprehensive mental health system. Interaction between the hospital and the community services will be necessary well before the patient is released, and must continue after he is discharged. Social workers, psychologists and occupational therapists are an important part of the *'resocialisation team'*. Their job is to help the person to be prepared for life outside the structured environment of the hospital. In the community the patient will need a home, a livelihood, recreation, continued treatment, care and support, and often nursing. The hospital can help by *'out-reach'* into the community through outpatient and day-patient services, community psychiatric and nursing services and liaison with other bodies. An important role must also be played by social services and the probation service. Through coordination, the expertise gained from the in-patient care of difficult patients can be shared while a range of community treatment facilities is developed. Using hospital staff in the community would also serve to lessen their isolation and the inward-looking approach which they can easily develop; and the patient would be more comfortable knowing that persons with whom he has a good relationship would continue to take a close interest in his welfare. To help in the development of an integrated approach, it would be useful to invite the local services to appoint *liaison officers* who would spend some of their time in the hospital forming relationships with staff and patients.

In summary, three agencies have responsibility for community services – health authorities, local authorities and the probation service. Each has an inbuilt motivation to try to place responsibility for a particular individual on another agency; by so doing, they avoid overloading their stretched facilities. The fact that different facilities are provided from different budgets, under separate managerial and administrative structures, constantly bedevils the rational allocation of resources to mentally disordered people, and prevents proper planning for a comprehensive mental health service.

Future secure provision for mentally disordered people requires no less careful planning to achieve a comprehensive and integrated service than any other aspect of mental health. Yet for too long the simple answer has been another locked ward or another secure unit. This report is intended to encourage a planned alternative policy.

Planning for secure provision for mentally handicapped people

For the last ten years and more there has been a great deal of planning of services for mentally handicapped people by government (for example, DHSS 1971, 1980) and by independent bodies (Independent Development Council for People with Mental Handicap 1982). The trend has been towards de-institutionalisation by providing for all the basic needs of mentally handicapped people in the community – housing, education, training, habilitation, social support and, where necessary, special medical, psychiatric or nursing provision. The phasing out of large mental handicap hospitals has been planned for some time now but it is being implemented only in the most inappropriate and remote institutions.

There is, however, one aspect of the care and treatment of mentally handicapped people that has not been examined at all – the small group who are potentially difficult or dangerous. It is important to recognise at once that mental handicap alone does not *cause* dangerous behaviour. But any person, whether mentally handicapped or not, may have potentially dangerous propensities by virtue of an accompanying mental illness or simply because of his or her character (sometimes labelled psychopathic disorder or behaviour disorder).

At the moment, a mentally handicapped person who is thought to be difficult or dangerous is often simply confined in a prison, special hospital, or in a locked ward of a local hospital. The plight of these people has seldom been brought to the attention of the public.

Moreover, because the numbers are relatively small, this state of affairs has had a degree of resigned acceptance from mental handicap professionals and even voluntary organisations. Yet few aspects of the mental health services are more cruel or inhumane than to surround a mentally handicapped person with security and to deny him an intensive programme of habilitation. The world of locked doors, physical and pharmaceutical restraint and occasional seclusion is not understood by a mentally handicapped person, who will have little hope of ever leaving it.

The problem manifests itself particularly in three places – prisons, special hospitals and local hospitals. At the last census returns (31 March 1984) there were 25 prisoners classified as severely mentally impaired, or mentally impaired, who were formally awaiting transfer to the NHS (Birmingham 1984). Other mentally handicapped people in the prison system are not officially on the transfer list, but their number is unknown.

The special hospitals are the major problem, because a significant proportion of their patients waiting for transfer to less secure local hospitals are mentally handicapped. At 31 December 1983, 233 special hospital patients were waiting to be transferred, of which 34 per cent were classified as severely mentally impaired or mentally impaired: indeed, the majority of those who had been waiting for two years or more were in these categories (DHSS 1984). Some had been on the transfer list for many years – for over four years or more. Staff on the wards of Rampton and Moss Side Hospitals will freely admit that most of their mentally handicapped population pose no real danger to themselves or others, and have not done so for a very long time. In one case a young woman was admitted to Moss Side some twenty years ago for a reason that the staff cannot even document; they believe it was because she had had a temper tantrum in a local hospital, damaging some curtains. To their knowledge the woman has never been dangerous to anyone, but her local hospital has persistently refused to have her. This woman is not unique. MIND estimated that at least two thirds of the mentally handicapped people in special hospitals should be transferred immediately.

Given that most mentally handicapped people in secure provision in the NHS do not exhibit seriously dangerous or socially irresponsible behaviour, it is reasonable to assume that they cannot be classified as suffering from mental impairment within the meaning of section 1 of the Mental Health Act 1983. The term 'mental impairment' in the Mental Health (Amendment) Act 1982 replaces 'sub-normality' which was used in the Mental Health Act 1959. The reason for the change was a recognition that only people of 'abnormally aggressive or seriously irresponsible conduct' could be classified as mentally impaired under contemporary mental health legislation, and thus be liable for long term compulsory detention in hospital. (For the background to the change in terminology, see Gostin 1978, 1983.) This change in terminology is of particular importance to special hospital patients since in law only detained patients can reside in the special hospitals. It is suggested that a large proportion of mentally handicapped people in special hospitals are not suffering from mental impairment and that legally they should not be there. In 1982 when the Mental Health (Amendment) Act was passed, the Secretary of State for Social Services gave an undertaking to the Independent Development Council for Mentally Handicapped People (IDC) and to MIND that there would be a systematic re-evaluation of all mentally handicapped people in special hospitals to determine if they fitted the definition of mental impairment. Clearly this re-evaluation has not taken place on a wide scale. In response to a parliamentary question (Parliamentary debates 1984a) the Under-Secretary of State for Social Services, Mr John Patten, said that there had not been a comprehensive re-assessment of detained mentally handicapped patients to see whether they could be classified as mentally impaired. He said there would be no classification for restricted patients. While the Act does not formally require this it would be quite wrong for a restricted patient to remain in a special hospital if he does not come within one of the four categories of mental disorder. As for unrestricted patients, the Minister said they would be re-assessed on the occasion of renewal of detention and when they appeared before a Mental Health Review Tribunal (Parliamentary debates 1984a). This is far from the undertaking originally given to IDC and MIND and does not approach the problem of unnecessary deprivation of liberty in a special hospital as a matter of urgency.

The DHSS has seen the transfer of mentally handicapped people to local hospitals as an 'administrative problem' to be solved without removing the autonomy of local hospitals to decide who they will take. While this is understandable, it fails to take into account that mentally handicapped people should have the right to care and habilitation in the least restrictive and most normal environment appropriate to their needs. The mentally handicapped person who waits in despair for a transfer from a special to a local hospital should have rights which the DHSS should enforce. The Secretary of State already has the power of enforcement under section 123 of the Mental Health Act 1983, which allows him to direct the transfer of patients from special to local hospitals. He has *never* exercised this power.

The final place where potentially difficult or dangerous mentally handicapped people are confined is on locked wards of local hospitals. At the end of 1982 there were 743 secure beds in local mental handicap hospitals. There is a wide variation of purpose and type of locked ward in this figure. For many hospitals it involves simply the locking of doors and the use of more obvious forms of security, such as physical restraint and seclusion. The National Development Team for Mentally Handicapped People have found highly inadequate conditions of care in many secure mental handicap wards; the staffing ratios were far too low and there were insufficient resources to provide an intensive habilitative environment. Sometimes a behaviour modification technique, 'time out' in a closed single room or a 'time out' box, is used inappropriately purely as a way of secluding the patient because he is disruptive and there are insufficient staff to occupy him fully (DHSS 1980a). Clearly a mentally handicapped person cannot understand, and suffers disproportionately from, long periods of seclusion or physical restraint. The more intrusive and punitive forms of restraint can have no place in the care of mentally handicapped people. An obvious example was the case of Nicki who, because he was hyperactive and there were insufficient staff to look after him, was tied to a post. The usual reason for confining mentally handicapped patients in local hospitals is not to meet their own needs, but staff shortage, inadequate training and guidance for staff, and lack of resources.

Despite the confinement of mentally handicapped people in unsuitable forms of secure provision there has been very little planning of how best to provide care for potentially difficult or dangerous patients. The regional secure unit programme was proposed as a rather simplistic solution to the inappropriate placing of mentally disordered people in prisons and special hospitals. But the DHSS said from the earliest stages of the regional secure unit programme (DHSS 1974a) that the units were not for mentally handicapped patients. (Regretfully, two units, one at Borocourt Hospital,

Reading, and one at Fieldhead Hospital, Wakefield, are for mentally handicapped people.) The DHSS has never said what form of secure provision is appropriate for mentally handicapped people. Clearly the maximum security conditions in prisons and special hospitals are wrong. Further the DHSS has long expressed a policy of phasing out large remote mental handicap hospitals, and local hospitals generally have been starved of resources. This makes it virtually impossible for local hospitals to provide the high staffing and other facilities necessary for constructive unobtrusive forms of security.

In sum, the DHSS, while recognising a major problem, has simply not planned a constructive solution. It is recommended that the DHSS form a high level working party on the same lines as the Glancy committee to examine the secure provision needs of mentally handicapped people throughout the NHS. In the absence of a positive response from government it is to be hoped that one of the major voluntary organisations concerned with mental handicap, such as the IDC or MENCAP will take a lead. The need for careful planning is not manifested in the numbers of people involved, rather it is in the human suffering and unnecessary deprivation of liberty for perhaps the most vulnerable and isolated section of our society, those mentally handicapped offenders and mentally handicapped people who are potentially disruptive and are, for the most part, not wanted in the NHS.

CHAPTER SEVEN

The protection of staff: powers of restraint and search

Any kind of hospital or home which cares for mentally ill or mentally handicapped people may, from time to time, have to exercise some degree of physical management and control. Yet, textbooks seldom give guidance as to the rights and responsibilities of persons exercising force over mentally disordered people (a noteworthy exception is Hoggett 1985). The questions that arise are not merely academic, they are profoundly important in a practical sense for mental health professionals. If a nurse seeks to control difficult or violent behaviour, to what extent does the law justify restraint, seclusion or search? If there is a management problem on a ward caused by a shortage of well-trained staff, what powers are there to lock a door, for example, to prevent an elderly wandering patient from walking out? These and many other similar situations are so familiar to psychiatrists, social workers and nurses that it is remarkable that there is so little detailed guidance about their rights and duties in law. This chapter examines the legal position of people who may have occasion to restrain, seclude or search mentally disordered persons.

Battery and assault

Under the common law any direct and intentional application of force to another person without lawful justification is a *battery*. Reasonable fear or apprehension of the unjustified use of force is an *assault*. The slightest unwanted contact is a battery; there need not be any substantial injury. Further, even if the intention behind the use of force is beneficial, it will be a battery unless there is a lawful justification. Lord Devlin (1962) once said that the common law 'does not consider that an act done without a person's consent but for his benefit is deserving of reward or even immunity from legal action. The Good Samaritan is a character unesteemed by the English law.'

A battery would result from any handling of a mentally disordered person by force unless it was justified, for example, by the person's consent. A battery could occur if a mentally disordered person were controlled or restrained by any direct means – for example, the application of personal or bodily force, mechanical restraints or sedation. Removing a patient forcibly to a room (even at a special hospital) can amount to a battery (*Pountney v Griffiths* 1975); so too would the forcible search of a person. An assault would result if a mentally disordered person had a reasonable fear or apprehension of the use of unlawful force – for example, if a doctor or nurse threatened to restrain a patient by conspicuously preparing an injection. (*Townley v Rushworth* 1964.)

False imprisonment

False imprisonment is the total and unlawful restraint of a person's liberty or movements, whether by constraining him from leaving a particular place, or compelling him to go to it. Confining a person in a hospital, a residential care home or even in his own home, without lawful justification is false imprisonment; so too is continuing to confine a person once the authority for detention has expired. The barriers need not be physical, so long as a show of force is used. Usually when there is a false imprisonment there is also an assault or battery, although this is not so, for example, where a person voluntarily enters a hospital ward which is subsequently locked. Besides bringing a claim in tort (that is, for damages) a person who is falsely imprisoned has the remedy of *habeas corpus*, which is used to obtain the release of anyone unlawfully confined. It is sometimes said that a person must actually be aware at the time that his liberty has been removed (*Herring v Boyle* 1834), but if this were true it would leave some mentally disordered people without a remedy. For example, a severely mentally handicapped or an elderly senile patient in hospital informally may not realise that he is being deprived of his liberty when locked in a room. The preferred view is that of Lord Justice Atkin in *Meering v Graham-White Aviation Co.* (1919): '. . . a person can be imprisoned while he is asleep, while he is in a state of drunkenness, while he is unconscious, and while he is a lunatic.'

Offences

Assault, battery and false imprisonment are not only civil torts for which damages can be awarded, but criminal offences. Generally the definitions are the same in crime as in tort.

Mental health legislation also provides for a number of specific criminal offences. Section 127 of the Mental Health Act 1983 makes it an offence for any member of staff, officer or manager of a hospital or mental nursing home to ill-treat or wilfully to neglect a patient. A single act such as slapping the patient's face on one occasion can be ill-treatment under section 127 (*R v Holmes*1979).

Section 128 of the Mental Health Act 1959 (which is still in force) makes it an offence to have sexual intercourse with patients.

Negligence

Anyone who has the responsibility for caring for or supervising a mentally disordered person must ensure that he does not do foreseeable harm to others (*Home Office v Dorset Yacht Co Ltd* 1970). If a person is detained in hospital, staff must take reasonable care to prevent his escape if it can be foreseen that, by escaping, he would cause harm to himself or others. Reasonable care must also be taken to prevent any foreseeable harm being caused by one patient to another. It is important to emphasise that hospital staff are not liable simply because harm is done by the patient; it must be proved that he failed to take the kind of reasonable care that other members of his profession would take (for example, he fell asleep while on duty).

What is the position if a doctor exercises a statutory responsibility by discharging a patient who then goes on to commit suicide or causes grave harm to others? The doctor is not liable for anything the patient does unless he was *grossly negligent* – for instance, by discharging a patient known to want to harm a close relative without warning the relative or taking steps to prevent the danger.

Justifications for the use of force

The law requires a person to have a legally recognised justification for the use of force against another person, even if the intention is benevolent (see Hoggett 1985). The most common justification is the person's consent. The Mental Health Act also grants specific powers which allow compulsion to be used against the will of a mentally disordered person. The use of force in the absence of consent and without an express justification under the Mental Health Act 1983 is most likely to cause those caring for mentally disordered persons to be uncertain of their legal rights and responsibilities. Unfortunately, staff must rely on a number of substantially overlapping and vague powers in the common law (now partly replaced by the Criminal Law Act 1967).

Consent

Consent is usually a justification for the use of force under the common law. A patient may, for example, request a private room or seclusion (or 'time out') as part of a general programme of behaviour modification. Consent can be given expressly, by words or in writing; or it can be implied by gestures, conduct or the absence of any resistance to an act ordinarily expected in the course of a professional/patient relationship. A patient may, in refutation of a suggestion that he is a thief, open his pockets as an invitation to be searched; if he then passively submits to the search that would probably constitute consent. Further, a consent – even if it is in writing – can be withdrawn at any time by the patient, for example, where the patient agrees to a period of seclusion but later asks to be let out.

For consent to be effective it must have a number of elements:

1 *Information*
   There is no doctrine of 'informed consent' in England and Wales, but in order to consent the patient must understand the broad nature and purpose of the restraint. (*Sidaway v Bethlem Royal Hospital* 1984). By entering the hospital informally, a patient may have implicitly agreed to the reasonable restraint necessarily entailed in the operation of the hospital – for example, limiting visiting hours or locking the doors of a ward at night. The patient, therefore, should be informed, in broad terms, of the hospital's internal rules. However, since he can withdraw consent at any time, he can, for example, demand that a locked door be opened to allow him to leave when he wishes.

2 *Voluntariness*
   Consent cannot be obtained by force or by a show of authority. For example, a nurse commanding an informal patient to enter a seclusion room or to submit to a personal search is no consent at all. The threat of compulsory admission made to an informal patient who decides to leave hospital or not to follow the advice of staff, could undermine the patient's free choice. However, if there were real grounds for the threatened action (that is, the patient's condition actually comes within the statutory criteria for compulsory admission) the patient's consent to the restraint might be upheld (*Buckland v Buckland* 1967). Whether a patient can give a voluntary consent depends upon the facts; there is no

rule of law saying that a patient can never consent of his own free will because of the institutional pressures upon him (*Freeman v Home Office* 1984).

3 *Competency*

The law's protection of the self-determination of the individual is founded almost entirely upon his ability to make a competent decision. Yet surprisingly little attention has been given by the courts in providing guidance about the competence of a person. What must the patient understand in order to be competent? It is generally thought that he must only be able to understand the broad nature and effects of the act. There is no rule of law which would preclude a patient from consenting because of his diagnosis or legal status. Further, competency is not an all-or-nothing concept. A patient's competency may vary over time or according to the act in question. The question must be put in each case – can he broadly understand the nature and effect of the act in question.

Substitute consent by the nearest relative

It is important to note that if a person cannot give consent (because he is not competent or the consent is involuntary) then consent cannot justify the use of force. In such cases the force may constitute a battery. The *nearest relative cannot* give consent on behalf of a patient. The only exception may be the parent or lawful guardian (*not* a Mental Health Act guardian) of a minor. Although a nearest relative has no power in law to consent on behalf of a patient it is, wherever possible, good professional practice to consult with and seek the agreement of the nearest relative before the use of restraint.

Medical treatment

The administration of *medical treatment* without consent can be justified under part IV of the Mental Health Act 1983. In general the 1983 Act allows a doctor to administer treatment to any patient compulsorily detained in hospital under a section which allows detention for 28 days or more. If drugs (after their use for three months) or electro convulsive therapy (ECT) are to be administered, the doctor needs the patient's consent *or* a second opinion. If psychosurgery or sex hormone treatment is to be used then the doctor needs the patient's consent *and* a second opinion. The administration of medical treatment is beyond the scope of this book and the reader is referred to other texts (Gostin 1983; Gostin 1985) for a full explanation.

It is, however, important to recognise that often there is a fine line between 'treatment', 'control' and 'management'. Simply because a procedure is under a doctor's supervision does not mean it is medical treatment governed by part IV of the Mental Health Act 1983. For example, injecting a major tranquilliser or secluding the patient in order to restrain and control him should be viewed, it is suggested, in the same way as physical or mechanical restraint, not as medical treatment.

The doctrine of 'necessity'

One of the most important questions for mental health professionals is how a permanently incompetent mentally disordered person can be restrained (if at all). Illustrations common to most mental hospitals are whether a door can be locked to prevent a senile wandering elderly patient from leaving the hospital; or whether a severely mentally handicapped patient can take part in a programme of behaviour modification which involves the administration of an aversive (that is, painful or unpleasant) stimulus or restraint? The doctrine of 'necessity' may, in certain circumstances, provide a justification for proceeding without consent. Plainly, restraint that is immediately necessary to preserve life can be used if the person's behaviour is involuntary. Should the senile patient previously referred to be about to wander (unsupervised and oblivious to the danger) onto a busy public road, a nurse could undoubtedly restrain him. This would not apply, of course, in the case of a patient who, although perhaps not fully aware of all of the dangers, was able to express an objection to the restraint by words or conduct. More importantly, it seems clear that if a door is locked to protect *one* patient from imminent harm, it is likely to constitute false imprisonment for the majority of the other patients who would not come to immediate harm if they left the ward.

The scope of the doctrine of necessity is uncertain and any case would probably turn on its facts. Relevant considerations would include whether the person is likely to regain competency (if he will regain competency force should be delayed whenever possible until he is in a position to consent); whether the danger is serious and immediate (force cannot be used unless the danger is imminent);

whether the restraint used is necessary and not merely convenient (force cannot be used for administrative convenience or for general management purposes); and whether the force used was reasonably necessary (the force must be the minimum amount needed to prevent an immediate danger). *Thus, the doctrine of necessity would probably provide sufficient protection for a member of staff who used reasonable force which was immediately necessary to prevent an incompetent patient from coming to any obvious and significant harm.*

The lack of guidance in the Mental Health Act or from the courts places members of staff in an invidious position. They have no assurance that they are protected in making difficult day-to-day decisions while controlling disruptive, dangerous or wandering patients. In particular, they have no clear advance notice as to how such concepts as 'competency', 'immediacy', 'reasonableness' and 'necessity' might be construed by a court after the fact.

Where consent is not a defence – abetting suicide or mercy killing

The overriding public policy of preventing crime is such that consent is not necessarily a defence to an unlawful act. The general principle is that it is unlawful to use such a degree of force that bodily harm is a probable consequence. A patient could not, for example, consent to a beating, even if he voluntarily entered into a fight with a member of staff or with another patient (*Attorney-General's Reference (No 6 of 1980)* 1981).

It is a specific statutory offence to aid, abet, counsel or procure a suicide or attempted suicide (Suicide Act 1961, section 2(1)). It is also an offence to kill by consent (that is, mercy killing). The motives in assisting a person in chronic pain to take his own life, or mercy killing, may be benign, but the patient's agreement will not provide a defence in law.

Justifications for the use of force under the Mental Health Act 1983

There are a large number of provisions in the Mental Health Act 1983 which allow the use of force without the person's consent. Generally speaking, the Mental Health Act does *not* provide a justification for the use of force *before an application for compulsory admission is duly completed* or before a doctor's or nurse's holding power is duly exercised. If access is required to a person's home for the purpose of a social work interview or medical examination, a magistrates' warrant must be obtained under section 135(1). However, *after an application for compulsory admission is duly completed* (that is, founded upon the requisite medical recommendations) the Act provides authority for the person's conveyance to hospital (section 6(1)). When a person is *actually compulsorily admitted to hospital on behalf of the managers* there is power to detain him for a period specified under the Mental Health Act (section 6(2)).

Any person authorised to be conveyed to any place or kept in custody or detained in a place of safety is deemed to be *'under legal custody'* (section 137). If such a person escapes he can be retaken by specified persons – by an approved social worker or by a member of staff (section 138). Any person who is absent from hospital without leave (or a guardianship patient who is absent without leave from a place he is required to reside) can also be retaken (section 18). If a patient who is liable to be retaken is in his own home, and is refusing entry to those authorised to recapture him, an application for a warrant should first be made under section 135(2) before entering the premises by force. (It is important to observe that there are time-limits set for the re-taking of patients and any use of force after the time has expired may constitute a battery or false imprisonment.) These powers under the Mental Health Act 1983 are examined in much greater detail in Gostin (1985) and Hoggett (1984).

Constraining a detained patient within the confines of the hospital

If an *informal* patient is locked in a room, placed in seclusion or prevented from leaving the hospital without lawful justification it is a false imprisonment. Under what circumstances can a *compulsorily* detained patient be secluded, locked in a room or otherwise restrained? It is sometimes assumed that once a person is compulsorily detained under the Mental Health Act, all forms of 'lesser' constraints within the hospital premises, or the withdrawal of ordinary rights, can be applied. But this is not necessarily so. If the Mental Health Act is to be used as a justification, any restraint of a detained person in hospital must be based upon what the Act says or necessarily implies. The House of Lords in *Pountney v Griffiths* (1975) said that compulsory detention must involve the exercise of 'control and discipline'. Thus any reasonable form of control and discipline which is necessary for the health, safety or medical treatment of a compulsorily detained patient would probably be upheld by the courts. However there could be no authority for the use of force for purposes not intended by the Act, such as for revenge or

143

punishment. Further, the use of force even for proper purposes must be reasonable in the circumstances; excessive or unnecessary force could not be justified. However, hospital staff are not required to make 'fine' judgments about the use of force in cases of emergency, and courts are likely to construe such concepts as 'reasonableness' in favour of hospital staff (see further below).

Preventing harm as a justification for the use of force

There are a whole variety of justifications for the use of force which are available to anybody (not necessarily members of hospital staff) to prevent a person from causing immediate harm. The four most important justifications are:

1 *Prevention of crime*

The Criminal Law Act 1967 (section 2) creates a category of more serious offences, termed 'arrestable offences', for which citizens have the power of arrest without warrant. Section 3(1) of the 1967 Act allows a person to use reasonable force either in making an arrest or in the prevention of crime. Unquestionably this would allow any private person to use reasonable force to prevent a crime which is actually in progress or is about to be committed; but it would not justify retaliation or punishment of a person who has already committed an offence. It would, for example, allow a nurse to restrain a patient who is about to do imminent harm to other persons or to property; or to restrain a patient who has taken, or who is about to take, property belonging to another patient or to the hospital. However, it would not justify placing a person in seclusion as punishment after he has committed a crime. There are several difficulties with the concept of 'committing a crime' under the Criminal Law Act. Since suicide is not a crime, could a person be prevented by force from committing suicide? Further, if a patient is so mad as not to be capable of understanding what he was doing or that it was unlawful (that is, he was insane under the M'Naghten Rules), he cannot technically commit a crime. It is certain that in both of these examples reasonable force could be used to prevent the patient from causing immediate harm to himself, to others or to property. However the justification would probably be found in the common law as opposed to the Criminal Law Act 1967.

2 *Prevention of breach of the peace*

Any person in whose presence a breach of the peace is committed, or who reasonably assumes it is being committed, can use reasonable force to make the person breaching the peace refrain from doing so (*Albert v Lavin* 1981). At common law this is not only the right of the person, it is a duty. There is a breach of the peace whenever harm is actually done or is likely to be done to a person or, in his presence, to his property; or where a person is in fear of being so harmed through an assault, an affray, a riot, unlawful assembly or other disturbance (*R v Howell* 1981). Thus, some harm (whether actual, likely or feared) is required for a breach of the peace. A patient whose words or behaviour are such that imminent violence is expected on a hospital ward would come within this definition; and a nurse (or even a fellow patient) is entitled to take reasonable steps to make the person refrain from breaching or threatening to breach the peace.

3   *Self-defence*
Self-defence in legal texts is sometimes referred to as a 'private defence' because it is not restricted to defence of oneself. This would surely justify a nurse going to the defence of a patient being assaulted by a fellow patient. However, as an assault is a crime, and defending against it is the prevention of crime, it is probable that a court would use the Criminal Law Act 1967 as justification. Self-defence can be used to ward off or prevent unlawful force and to avoid or escape from unlawful detention. (A person defending himself need not wait until a blow is struck, but can take reasonable steps to prevent a patient from causing harm.) A nurse could, under this doctrine, take all reasonable measures to ensure that she does not come to harm. Courts used to speak of the 'duty to retreat', particularly before using extreme force. However, this common law duty has now been cast in *R v Julien* (1969) as a 'willingness to disengage': 'what is necessary is that he should demonstrate by his actions that he does not want to fight. He must demonstrate that he is prepared to temporise and disengage and perhaps to make some physical withdrawal.' Reasonable force can be used to defend oneself from an innocent aggressor, such as a person who is insane under the M'Naghten Rules. This is of importance to a staff member protecting himself against an attack by a seriously mentally disordered person.

4   *Restraining a dangerously mentally ill person*
Lord Mansfield said long ago in the case of *Brookshaw v Hopkins*

(1790): 'God forbid, too, that a man should be punished for restraining the fury of a lunatic, when that is the case'. There is old authority that a person who is both a 'lunatic' and 'dangerous' may be restrained (*Scott v Wakem* 1862; *Symm v Fraser* 1863; see Lanham 1974 and Carson 1982). The person must, in fact, be mentally ill; a reasonable belief is probably insufficient (*Sinclair v Broughton* 1882; *Fletcher v Fletcher* 1859). This common law justification for restraining a 'dangerous lunatic' is very difficult to apply today. We have no definition which is equivalent to 'lunatic' as understood in the 18th and 19th centuries. The definition of 'mental disorder' in the Mental Health Act is too wide. If this justification could be relied upon at all today it would only be in relation to a seriously mentally ill person who was 'not in possession of his faculties' (*Fletcher v Fletcher* 1859).

Guidance for staff

The four justifications for the use of force to prevent harm which are set out above are often vague and overlapping. They do not provide sufficiently clear guidance to those caring for mentally disordered persons: carers will remain unclear as to the scope and limits of their *powers* to restrain patients and their *duties* to protect patients from harm to themselves or others. Must the staff member pause to consider whether suicide is a crime or whether the patient is technically 'M'Naghten mad'; whether a breach of the peace is reasonably threatened; or whether he is entitled to use self-defence?

To answer these questions as simply and constructively as possible for members of staff responsible for the day-to-day care of potentially difficult violent patients, it is helpful to discuss the four justifications as a whole. The various justifications can be summarised as a general principle: that *reasonable force can be used to prevent any person from acting in a manner which is likely to cause an imminent danger to himself, other persons or to property.* Powers of restraint probably may not be used where there is no immediate danger but only a general and unspecific concern about the health or safety of the patient.

'Reasonable in all the circumstances'

It is probable that a modern court would require the use of force, irrespective of the justification relied upon, to be reasonable in all the circumstances. (This is an express statutory requirement where the Criminal Law Act 1967 is to be relied upon.)

'Reasonable force' incorporates two concepts: the force must be *necessary* and it must be *proportionate* to the harm to be avoided. Only force which is necessary to prevent the harm is justified. If the harm could have been prevented without the use of force, or by lesser force, that course of action must be adopted. For example, if a patient can be verbally dissuaded from doing violence, that must be attempted.

Further, the *degree* and *duration* of the force must be proportionate to the harm to be prevented. For example, a nurse or doctor could not beat a patient or render him unconscious to prevent him from stealing property. Nor could a patient be secluded or placed into mechanical restraints for a period long after the immediate danger has passed; the use of force must be the least necessary to bring the harm or threatened harm to an end. It is possible that, in relation to minor offences (for example, stealing a spoon from the canteen), *no* force could be used reasonably. The member of staff must ask these questions: is it reasonable to use force at all; what is the least amount of force which is necessary to accomplish the objective; when realistically will the danger be over and force discontinued? The member of staff should seek to avoid or to minimise the use of force so as not to cause the patient any unnecessary injury; *punishment, retaliation or excessive force cannot be justified.*

As a general rule a member of staff is well advised not to rely upon the Criminal Law Act 1967 or the common law to justify the use of force or restraint when there is sufficient opportunity and means to have recourse to specified powers in the Mental Health Act. For example, if it is necessary to lock a door without the patient's consent, an emergency application for compulsory admission under section 4 should, wherever appropriate, be used; or if it is necessary temporarily to restrain an informal patient until an application for compulsory admission can be completed, resort should, wherever possible, be made to the doctor's or nurse's holding power under section 5 of the Act.

The making of 'fine judgments' is not necessary

The member of staff exercising force, particularly in an emergency, is not expected to make a fine calculation: 'Detached reflection cannot be demanded in the presence of an uplifted knife' (*Brown v the United States*, dictum of Justice Holmes). The concept of reasonableness is intended to prevent gross overreaction – that is, force of a severity or duration which no reasonable person would be expected to use in the circumstances.

Clearly even this guidance begs a number of critical questions – in particular what is 'reasonable in the circumstances'; or what kind of force, and for how long must it be applied to be regarded as 'proportionate'. A nurse who cares for seriously mentally ill or mentally handicapped people, day after day, deserves detailed advice and guidance, both professional and legal. It would be terribly unfair for a member of staff to take a decision in good faith and then to be told by a court reviewing the case after the fact that it was unlawful. (But see section 139 of the Mental Health Act 1983 which protects any person acting in pursuance of that Act so long as he did so in good faith and with reasonable care – see below.)

It is recommended that:

1 The courts should take the earliest opportunity to provide guidance as to the law where force may have to be used by those caring for patients.

2 In the longer term Parliament should consider whether to clarify the law. It is essential, however, not to provide staff with any special privileges which have the effect of putting mental patients in a disadvantageous legal position. Thus any special protection for staff must not be achieved by diminishing the rights of patients. For example, a system of compensation for staff could be established (see below).

3 The DHSS should set up an inter-disciplinary working party to provide a detailed set of legal, professional and ethical guidelines for staff. Doctors, lawyers, nurses, social workers from outside the department should be recruited.

4 Alternative to 3 above, the Mental Health Act Commission should produce legal and professional guidelines for staff. It is expected that some guidelines will be produced in the forthcoming code of practice.

In laying down legal and professional guidelines the rights of the patient as well as the protection of staff must be considered.

Power to search patients

Searching a patient is no more than a particular kind of force and would be likely to be examined according to the rules previously discussed. Yet, search raises particular questions on which mental hospital staff need guidance. The issue arose in the House of Commons during the debates on the Mental Health (Amendment) Bill, but the Act still fails to provide guidance. The debates and the author's numerous discussions with hospital staff in the course of preparing this report, made it increasingly clear that there is widespread misunderstanding about the law relating to search of patients.

There are no watertight answers, but the following guidance can be given in relation to many of the issues which arise. It should be emphasised that a search of the person or his possessions can be highly intrusive and degrading, potentially undermining the patient's self-esteem and dignity. Search should be discouraged, professionally and legally, unless it is the least intrusive way of preventing serious harm.

General inspection of a patient's room

A general inspection of a patient's room for the purpose of observing whether it is clean or the bed is made is probably something to which the patient has implicitly consented when admitted to hospital. So long as his body, clothing or personal possessions were not touched it is doubtful whether the patient would have any cause of action in a court. However, any search of the patient himself or his personal possessions, in the absence of lawful justification, would be a battery.

Search for dangerous articles

Guidance in HC (76)11 (DHSS 1976) states that staff have authority at common law and by virtue of the Criminal Law Act 1967 to take reasonable measures to prevent a patient from keeping in his possession articles of danger such as matches, weapons, alcohol, tools and explosives. This overstates the nurse's legal powers. The nurse could only search for a dangerous article if there were reasonable grounds for believing i) that the person was in possession of the article, *and* ii) either that possession of the article itself was a crime or that the article is likely to be used for a crime. For example, if there were reasonable grounds to believe that matches were about to be used to set fire to a ward or string to be used to strangle a fellow patient, a search might well be justified. On the other hand, a general concern that matches or string should not be possessed would be unlikely to give rise to a justification for search of an informal patient. Arguably, even if an informal patient were alcohol dependent he could not be searched for alcohol unless its use could reasonably be expected to cause an immediate danger. Every case would have to be decided on its facts. The test would be whether there were reasonable grounds to believe a crime was about to be committed and whether a search was necessary and the least intrusive means of preventing a crime.

Search for stolen property

It is doubtful whether an informal patient could be searched for stolen goods. If there is a reasonable suspicion of theft, the person can be arrested, and taken before a justice of the peace or to a police station as soon as reasonably possible. The police or justice of the peace have the power to search in these circumstances.

Routine search

Staff in mental hospitals are not empowered to carry out a 'fishing expedition' or a routine search of patients in order simply to establish whether there is any possible risk of future harm. There must be individual and particular grounds for a search. It is, for example, common practice on some hospital wards to search a patient's clothing to discover whether he has taken a prescribed drug or whether he is in possession of alcohol. Without the patient's consent, such a search cannot be regarded as lawful.

Power to search detained patients

A legal text was quoted with approval by the Under-Secretary of State for Health, Mr Kenneth Clarke, in the parliamentary debates on the Mental Health (Amendment) Act: 'insofar as those in charge of a *detained* patient may do whatever is necessary for his well-being or for the safety of others, a search without his consent, e.g. for a knife or drugs would clearly be justified'. This probably overestimates the extent of legal powers of search. Nowhere in the Mental Health Act is there any express provision regarding search of detained patients. However, it can be safely assumed that if there is a reasonable belief that the patient has in his possession an instrument to enable him to abscond (a key or a rope), it can be seized. Also, the Act would probably allow search if there were reasonable cause to believe a detained patient was in possession of a potentially dangerous item, such as a knife or gasolene, even if there were no immediate risk of it being used. This appears to be within the powers of 'control and discipline' of detained patients as contemplated by the House of Lords in *Pountney v Griffiths* (1975). There is considerable doubt, however, whether 'control and discipline' would extend to general or routine search where there was no reasonable ground to believe the patient was in possession of an article which would endanger a person's health or safety.

Protection against acts done in pursuance of the Mental Health Act

Section 139 of the Mental Health Act 1983 provides considerable protection against litigation for any member of staff who performs a duty authorised under the Act. Civil proceedings cannot be brought against that person without the consent of the High Court, and criminal proceedings cannot be brought without the consent of the Director of Public Prosecutions. Further consent to bring an action will not be given unless the member of staff acted in bad faith or without reasonable care.

Mistake of fact: performing an act without actual authority

Section 139 provides protection for members of staff who act without authority while *thinking* they have authority; for instance, a nurse who restrains a patient whom she reasonably, but wrongly, believes to be compulsorily detained. The nurse is protected so long as she acted in good faith and with reasonable care. 'If a person is acting honestly with the intention of performing, in the best way he knows how, the statutory functions or duties which are cast upon him, ... then he is acting in purported pursuance of the statute' (*Ashingdane v Secretary of State for Social Services and Others* 1980, per Bridge, LJ).

Mistake in law

What if a member of staff makes an honest mistake in law; for example, a doctor or nurse who restrains or treats an informal patient without consent in the belief that it is lawful? Could a person be mistaken in law and still act with reasonable care? Apparently, the answer is yes. In *Richardson v LCC* (1957) the court said: '... provided the statute could, in the mind of a person who is not a lawyer, reasonably be thought to bear that construction, it cannot be said that he has acted without reasonable care'. A member of staff should take steps to apprise himself of the law, but if he makes an honest mistake, which any of his colleagues might have made, he may still be protected by section 139.

Acts provided for in the statute

The courts have construed section 139 very widely. It clearly protects staff (and any other person) in respect of acts expressly provided for in the Mental Health Act, such as signing an application or medical recommendation for compulsory admission. It also applies to any act necessarily implied in the Act. In *Pountney v Griffiths* (1975) the House of Lords quoted Lord Widgery with approval: 'where a male nurse is on duty and exercising his functions of controlling the patients in the hospital, acts done in pursuance of such control . . . are acts within the scope of section 149 [now section 139], and are thus protected'.

Informal patients

It is important to observe, however, that the foregoing applies only to detained patients. It is very doubtful whether section 139 provides any protection to hospital staff in their day-to-day management of informal patients (see *R v Runighian* 1977).

Policy

Section 139 does not protect staff where there is, perhaps, the most ambiguity, in their relationship with informal patients. However, in providing some protection for staff, section 139 removes one of the most fundamental rights of the patient. Most patients – even if compulsorily detained – do not bring vexatious or groundless cases to the courts, any more than the population at large. Indeed the exceedingly few instances where leave has been requested to bring a case under section 139 and its predecessors shows that most patients are very reticent about pursuing even their rightful claims in a court of law. It is quite wrong that any patient – merely by entry into a mental hospital – may lose his right to use the courts without impediment.

It is proposed that section 139 is abolished and replaced with a constructive protection for members of staff in relation to any act done in the course of their employment in good faith and with reasonable care. It should not matter whether the patient is informal or detained since it is the staff member who is to have protection, not the patient who is to have his rights removed.

Patients should have the same right to use the courts of law as any other citizen. But staff should be defended by their employer (the health authority) who should pay their costs in relation to any action concerned with their employment, and any damages in cases where a member of staff has acted in good faith and with reasonable care.

It may, however, be reasonable for section 139 to continue to apply to criminal proceedings, for it would be unfair for a member of staff to pay a criminal penalty when he has acted in good faith and with reasonable care. This is a matter where it is to be hoped that the DPP will protect the interests of patients as well as staff.

Summary of recommendations: The protection of staff

Guidance for staff

1 *The courts should take the earliest opportunity to clarify the legal principles involved where force may have to be used by those caring for patients.*

2 *In the longer term, Parliament should consider whether it is necessary to clarify the law. It is essential, however, not to provide staff with special privileges which have the effect of putting mental patients in a disadvantageous legal position. Thus any special protection must not be achieved by diminishing the rights of patients.*

3 *The DHSS should set up an inter-disciplinary working party to provide a detailed set of legal, professional and ethical guidelines for staff in the management of potentially difficult or dangerous patients.*

4 *As an alternative to 3, the Mental Health Act Commission should produce legal and professional guidelines for staff.*

Search

5 *Search is a personally intrusive form of restraint and should be used only when it is the least intrusive way in which to prevent an immediate and serious danger to health or safety.*

Protection of staff

6 *Section 139 of the Mental Health Act 1983 should be abolished and replaced with a constructive protection for members of staff.*

7 *Staff should have special protection in any case where they have acted in the course of their employment; it should not matter whether the patient concerned is of an informal or compulsory legal status.*

   a) *in such a case, staff should be defended in court by their employer (the relevant health authority) with all their costs paid;*

b) *if the member of staff has acted in good faith and with reasonable care any damages awarded should be paid by the employer.*

8 *It is reasonable for section 139 to continue to apply to criminal proceedings, for it would be unfair for a member of staff to pay a criminal penalty if he acted in good faith and with reasonable care. This is a matter where it is to be hoped that the DPP will protect the interests of patients as well as staff.*

COMMENTARY
BY VISCOUNT COLVILLE OF CULROSS

A new book by Larry Gostin is calculated to arouse interest and controversy. Nothing less can be expected of this publication. Secure accommodation for mentally disordered people is the concern of many professionals, but it also is a subject which causes concern to many members of the public. These two groups do not necessarily look at it from the same viewpoint.

It must be good to open up some of the arguments even when the Mental Health Act 1983 has hardly been in operation for two years. Some would say that the reforms in it took place too long after the last major reform in 1959. Nor is it at all certain that every problem has been correctly resolved by the Act's provisions. This book, however, goes far beyond what was sought to be achieved in the late 1970s and early 1980s. It would certainly need further major legislation and an accord between the Home Office and the DHSS which might be hard to achieve.

The book rightly stresses the concept of the least restrictive choice of a place for treatment for mentally disordered people. The pendulum has swung from a large measure of security to an approach which has opened the doors of very many hospitals, while leaving the special hospitals as secure as ever. We in the Mental Health Act Commission are watching with great interest the role now unfolding for the regional secure units. The idea, on which Mr Gostin expands, of much greater flexibility, both in terms of 'flexible security' and of more options for a patient's ideal placement, is extremely attractive. Whether it is achievable within the resources likely to be available is quite another matter; but for the patient and his family a range of hospital facilities, mostly not far from his home and tailored for each stage of his treatment and rehabilitation, must be an ideal worth striving for.

In that range the special hospitals must, and do, find their place. The chapter on these hospitals is very critical. The Mental Health Act Commission is also taking a close interest in them and would agree that improvements can and should be made. Indeed there is a constant effort to get to grips with some of the intangible problems

155

and seek solutions. This includes improving the systems so that complaints can be seen to be fully investigated in all their aspects. At this point, however, the book would undoubtedly fall foul of some very ancient concepts of the legal system, concepts which still have a substantial public following. Patients in the special hospitals are not all there because they have committed criminal offences, but many are: they were either mentally disordered at the time when they appeared in court or having been sentenced were subsequently found to be so and were transferred from prison. These will have been sentenced to a fixed or an indefinite term of imprisonment, and increasingly the courts look to the guideline cases as setting a tariff as the basis, at least, of the correct approach to sentencing. This is at present especially so for those sentenced to life imprisonment or for certain other serious crimes; despite any subsequent onset of mental disorder their sentence stands and will not lead to release on licence until a condign period has been served. The public safety aspect is also built into the 1983 Act in the way in which both Mental Health Review Tribunals and the Home Office respectively deal with patients under restriction. From this it is necessary to pass to the earlier stage at which the offender is being tried. It is bold indeed to suggest that, for example, a psychopathic offender should himself be allowed to choose between prison and hospital treatment (though the idea has been put forward before). A medical method of dealing with the offender is already open to both parties, and to the court; and there is the real problem of determining whether choice can be a realistic concept for the offender in the circumstances facing him. A fundamental problem, however, which occurs now, arises where a serious crime has been committed, hospital treatment is chosen and the patient proves to be untreatable. He cannot be given a substituted prison sentence, but his immediate release into the community is an unsavoury prospect.

The Prison Medical Service does not, of course, only deal with mentally disordered prisoners. Major physical treatments will take place in outside hospitals, but some prison hospitals can provide a wide range of services. Further than that, however, the hospital is often an integral part of the custodial facilities; how something of this nature could be maintained while handing over the medical aspects to the NHS is not addressed in the book, although it may soon be by a Parliamentary Select Committee.

Perhaps the way to approach the book's contents is to start at

Chapter 4, and come back to the initial chapters later. There may be a shift in philosophy and resources required before the more varied secure accommodation can be made available. A glance over the shoulder is also advisable since the next step could be to tackle the problem of the mentally disordered offender. For such a person a target of, say, eighteen months to be spent on a regional secure unit or in the local secure units as proposed, would leave an insurmountable obstacle in finding the next phase leading towards discharge, unless the 'risk to the public' consideration receives a radical downgrading. Such a shift runs contrary to much of what the public sees as its right to be protected. It could not be embarked upon unless the range of units offering some degree of security, though less than that in the special hospitals, were already in place; and all members of staff would have to appreciate that the medical presentation of a patient is not the only matter to be considered. There is a large educational task ahead; it is to be hoped that the decisions by the Mental Health Review Tribunals to use their new powers by way of discharging patients under restriction orders will prove to have been judiciously taken. Some experience of this must precede legislation to extend their powers to ordering a transfer between hospitals; and precede decisions further to empty the special hospitals by large scale transfers, whether of mentally ill or mentally impaired patients.

This is not just a reactionary view derived from old Home Office experience. Mr Gostin is right in attributing much current frustration to the block that confronts a patient in a special hospital, and so, too, those who are planning his rehabilitation. However, the concerns of two Departments are directly involved, and unhappily these are not always harmonised. Undoubtedly the judiciary, too, would welcome a greater range of facilities for those who come before the courts; but they would have to be satisfied that attitudes as well as régimes in the NHS hospitals are properly orientated.

In this book there is already questioning of difficult decisions reached only three years ago, such as that of the definition of severe mental impairment. Broadsides are fired in several directions against current practice and provision of facilities. Many seem to find their target, but that is because the targets are large, elderly and slow-moving. A reconsidered and redesigned strategy might leave much less at which to fire.

Viscount Colville of Culross
Chairman, Mental Health Act Commission

'Treatment under security': a special case of medical coercion

COMMENTARY BY DR T W HARDING

Larry Gostin's description of and comments on various forms of secure provision for mentally disordered persons highlights the ethical dilemmas which face doctors and other care providers who work in such settings. 'Treatment under conditions of security' implies a direct conflict with one of the basic tenets of medical practice: treatment should be freely consented by the patient. We are therefore concerned with an important exception to the ethical principles which apply to the relationship between doctors and patients; an exception which covers, as Larry Gostin shows, several thousands of people in the United Kingdom at any one time. This example of medical coercion and of medical involvement in social control can obviously lead to major abuses such as the 'political' misuse of psychiatry in the Soviet Union (Bloch 1981) or the widespread and unjustified use of involuntary hospitalisation created by economic pressures in Japan (Harding and others 1985).

Most people are antipathetic about coercion. Exercising control over others implies authority and domination on the part of the controller and submission and suffering on the part of the controlled. In most human societies, social homeostasis is maintained largely through the caring, respect and mutual aid which characterises most social interactions. Psychiatry is often involved in social interventions with advice and support to families, various forms of crisis intervention, alleviation of various forms of psychopathology. These obviously can contribute to a form of 'social control without coercion' by preventing the acute episodes of decompensation in mentally ill persons which can lead to social disruptive behaviour and violence which, in turn, result in coercive forms of intervention by the police, the courts and the various forensic psychiatric services described by Larry Gostin.

Both in society as a whole and in the field of psychiatry, the social control provided by the police, by criminal justice and by other coercive measures is of secondary importance, except (and it is unfortunately an important exception) in the case of repressive and authoritarian regimes and when inadequate legal safeguards are provided for the protection of mentally ill persons.

It is therefore natural and reassuring that medicine as a whole and psychiatry in particular should be reluctant to resort to coercion in any form. The relationship between a patient and a doctor should be based on mutual respect and collaboration with an agreement about the interventions to be carried out. The patient *seeks* help because he is concerned or suffering. The doctor responds to the *patient's* request. The same principles hold for other groups of health personnel.

There are exceptions, however, to this ideal model of a freely consented relationship carried on under conditions of confidentiality and mutual respect. The most obvious exception occurs in the case of children who are brought to a doctor by their parents and receive treatments to which they manifestly do not consent. But more subtle pressures are often brought to bear by families, employers, schools, social workers and others. Patients often seek treatment not through their own initiative but to satisfy, placate or reassure their relatives or those on whom they are dependent.

Sylvia Plath, in her autobiographical novel *The Bell Jar* provides a telling description of such family pressures leading to hospitalisation and individual psychotherapy in the early phases of her depressive illness which was to end tragically in her suicide. There is no doubt that many 'voluntary' hospitalisations and ambulatory treatments are carried out under such subtle and hidden forms of pressure, including the implied threat to resort to coercion if the patient does not accept a treatment.

A much more dramatic exception occurs when it is not the family or the immediate social environment which provides the pressure, but the State. Clearly, the potential alliance between the State and medicine merits careful and critical examination. In my view, medical ethics is largely concerned with controlling and limiting this alliance. The point here has nothing to do with the debate between protagonists of socialised or liberal systems of health care, an essentially *political* issue. It has to do with moral values. All medical care should be directed towards health whether individual or collective. The State has other interests: public security, stability, economic growth, national prestige, responding to public opinion, however irrational. Medicine, whether operated in a socialised or a liberal system, must not become too closely identified with the State. Conflicts between the values implied in 'health' and the interests of the State can obviously occur and lead to actions which are not only against the human rights of individuals but even directly harmful to their physical and mental health.

Larry Gostin shows how such conflicts arise in the management of individuals thought to be both mentally ill *and* dangerous. But before discussing the issue of psychiatric treatment under secure conditions, which is undoubtedly the numerically most important example of coercion in medical care, it can be useful to look briefly at another example: the various forms of obligation which exist in the field of infectious disease control. This can provide us with a model of how conflicts arise between the interests of society as a whole and those of individuals and how these conflicts are handled.

Historically the exclusion of persons suffering from leprosy (Trautman 1984) and the practice of quarantine were the earliest forms of obligation – the former concerning patients with a chronic, disfiguring illness of low contagiosity and the latter aimed at prevention of epidemics imported from foreign lands. The roots of irrational reactions to unknown and unquantified dangers can be seen in these early practices.

The legal provisions vary from country to country. Pre-nuptial examinations are for example compulsory in Bulgaria, France and Luxembourg but not in most other European countries. In many countries, there has been a tendency to diminish the degree of obligation over the past ten years: the most notable example being the relaxation of obligatory controls and treatment for smallpox, following its eradication. In some instances obligation enforced by penal sanctions has been replaced by more subtle measures: in California, for example, non-vaccinated children cannot be admitted to public schools.

Nevertheless, in many countries provisions which are clearly discriminatory and violate the basic principles of medical ethics do exist. Liberty, the right to refuse treatment, the right to marry and various other fundamental rights are compromised by such measures, whose necessity in terms of public health is highly questionable (Moerloose 1961).

Today, medical interventions for the control of infectious diseases can still be legally enforced in a number of circumstances, for example:

a) compulsory medical examinations for immigrants, special groups of workers and those intending to marry;
b) compulsory vaccinations;
c) isolation of persons who have been in contact with certain infectious diseases;
d) treatment for certain conditions, which can mean hospitalisation, even if the patient does not consent.

The issue of coercion in relation to infectious illnesses has, of course, recently become topical and controversial in relation to governmental regulations concerning the control of AIDS.

The justification for obligatory medical interventions in the case of infectious diseases is, of course, the danger for the public represented by such diseases as tuberculosis, sexually transmitted diseases, 'exotic' diseases, and so on. The concept of danger here implies two elements: i) the degree of contagiosity – that is, the probability of diseases transmission; and, ii) the seriousness of the harmful effects produced by the disease: mortality rate, chronic effects and need for long-term treatment. The word danger thus encloses a double meaning: risk and seriousness. Athlete's foot is highly contagious but its consequences are minor. Leprosy has a very low rate of transmission, its consequences can be serious. Neither should be called 'dangerous' a term which should be reserved for conditions where *both* criteria are met.

We should also note that in the case of infectious diseases, the word 'dangerous' is applied normally to the *illness* not the *person*. This seems to me to be essential if one is to maintain a medical attitude in applying the concept of dangerousness to illnesses. It is when leprosy sufferers became labelled as dangerous *people* that unfair discrimination became widespread. The same risk now applies to AIDS sufferers. Once the label 'dangerous' is attached to a person and not to his condition and/or his environment, 'health' is no longer the prevailing value (with, of course, the possible conflict between individual and collective interests) and public security, much more difficult to define, takes its place.

The main implication of the infectious diseases/coercive measures model to the field of forensic psychiatry is the care which should be given in defining and applying the concept of dangerousness to people. It is somewhat disconcerting to find that Larry Gostin himself accepts from the outset the concept of '. . . dangerous, mentally disordered people . . .' in asking where such people should be placed.

161

Great care is needed in defining a term which is so semantically complex and affectively charged as 'dangerous'. Legal definitions do not appear to help in promoting rational and reliable use of the concept in clinical judgments (Beigel and others 1984). Nevertheless, inconsistent, muddled and uncritical use of the concept seems to be widespread among psychiatrists (Quinsey and Ambtman 1979; Montandon and Harding 1984). The unreliability of psychiatric assessments of dangerousness is probably a major factor in the serious lack of predictive value of such assessments, which has lead Steadman (1983) to suggest that psychiatrists function more like magicians than scientists in predicting violent behaviour.

Clear, operational definitions of dangerousness as applied to certain psychopathological states should be formulated and should form the basis for improved training for psychiatrists. The role of the psychiatrist in predicting dangerousness should be limited to cases of mental illness. The diagnostic criteria and the predictive factors are clearly established, but rarely applied in a consistent fashion. In the case of personality disorders, this is not the case and psychiatric assessment is of little or no predictive value. Life-time risk of violent behaviour may be increased in individuals with 'anti-social personality' according to DSM III criteria, but the risk is probably largely related to the secondary social handicaps which such people accumulate. The unsatisfactory definition of psychopathic disorder in the 1983 Mental Health Act is, of course, underlined by Larry Gostin. It would be preferable to eliminate it altogether.

The core of the problem is therefore to limit assessments of dangerousness:
a) in terms of a clear, semantic definition which includes both the *risk* of certain behaviours and the degree of *harm* which results. This allows many cases with the label 'dangerousness' to be relativised;
b) to cases of clearly established mental illness and excluding cases of personality disorder;
c) in terms of the duration of the prediction. Long term predictions are never possible because the evolution of a major mental illness is subject to considerable variation.

It follows that psychiatrists should be involved not so much in *assessing* dangerousness but in *managing* dangerousness as one clinical parameter in certain cases of severe mental disorder. Adequate management is possible only if adequate services are available. This is the crunch. This is where currently in Britain both patients and staff lose out. Despite the large amount of resources deployed, management choices remain much too restricted. Most secure provisions are available in the special hospitals which provide long term, custodial care which leads to institutionalisation and atrophy of existing community and social links, even when devoted and skilled staff do their best. Such secure hospitals exist in other countries but it seems that the number of beds provided is considerably higher in Britain than in most other European countries.

In other countries, notably Holland, it has been shown that even very difficult cases can be treated, sometimes over long periods, in small, decentralised, specialised units.

In this context I feel that Larry Gostin's lukewarm appraisal of the regional secure units in England is unfortunate. Of course, some of the models so far developed are deficient. Of course, there have been staffing and funding problems and a scandalously long gestation period. However, it is the first major breakthrough in forensic psychiatric services since Broadmoor was opened and it must surely be of benefit to patients. Staff training and morale have been dramatically improved and, without exception, regional programmes of outpatient treatment have been developed. This deserves wholehearted support and encouragement. It is only when manifestly competent and well organised forensic psychiatric services are developed on a *local* basis that we can avoid the 'sweeping under the carpet' solution practised for so many years. The best regional services are not afraid of admitting the limits of psychiatric care and of showing authorities (judicial and others) that a certain degree of risk must be tolerated in the community if unacceptable levels of coercive, custodial care are to be avoided.

Legal safeguards for mentally disordered people are essential. Larry Gostin shows how they are often deficient. However, the single most important factor in promoting the rights of the mentally ill (and especially of the minority who manifest periodically violent behaviour) is the availability of a range of treatments and services including secure provision in small, purpose built units and the provision of psychiatric care for prisoners who ask for it.

Therapeutic community approaches, drug treatment, individual psychotherapy, groups, family therapy, social interventions, counselling: all can be effective in helping patients whose illnesses have led them into conflict with society. None is likely to be effective on a significant scale without the framework of a differentiated, well staffed and trained forensic psychiatric service made available on a local basis.

Dr T W Harding
Head, Division of Forensic Psychiatry and Prison Medicine
University Institute of Legal Medicine
Geneva

REFERENCES

Albert R S, Brigante T R and Chase M (1959) The psychopathic personality: a content analysis of the concept. Journal of General Psychology 60: 17–28.

Ashworth A and Gostin L (1984) Mentally disordered offenders and the sentencing process. Criminal Law Review, April: 195–212.

Beigel A, Berren M R and Harding T W (1984) The paradoxical impact of a commitment statute on prediction of dangerousness. American Journal of Psychiatry 141: 373–377.

Bingley W and Gostin L (1985) A joint campaign for adequate and humane care and treatment of women prisoners with mental health problems in Holloway Prison. London, MIND-NCCL.

Birmingham J (1984) Personal correspondence from the Under-Secretary of State for Social Services.

Bloch S (1981) The political misuse of psychiatry in the Soviet Union. In: Bloch S and Chodoff P (eds) Psychiatric Ethics. Oxford, Oxford University Press: 323–341.

Bluglass R (1978) Regional secure units and interim security for psychiatric patients. British Medical Journal 1: 489–493.

Bluglass R (1985) The development of regional secure units. In: Gostin L (ed) Secure provision: a review of special services for the mentally ill and mentally handicapped in England and Wales. London, Tavistock Publications: 153–175.

Bowden P (1975) Liberty and psychiatry. British Medical Journal 4: 94–96.

Bowden P (1978) Men remanded into custody for medical reports: the selection for treatment. British Journal of Psychiatry 133: 320–331.

Bowden P (1985) Psychiatry and dangerousness: a counter renaissance? In: Gostin L (ed) Secure provision: a review of special services for the mentally ill and mentally handicapped in England and Wales. London, Tavistock Publications: 265–287.

Brody S and Tarling R (1980) Taking offenders out of circulation. Report. London, HMSO, Home Office Research Unit.

Carney M P W and Nolan P A (1978) Area security unit in a psychiatric hospital. British Medical Journal 1: 27–28.

Carson D (1982) Detention of the mentally disordered. Local Government Review 146: 887–890, 899.

Casales S (1985) Minimum prison standards. In: McGuire M, Vaag J and Morgan R (eds) Accountability and prisons: opening up a closed world. London, Tavistock Publications.

Cleckley H (1964) The mask of sanity. Fourth edition. St Louis, C V Mosby.

Cobb J P and Gossop M R (1976) Locked doors in the management of disturbed psychiatric patients. Journal of Advanced Nursing 1: 469–480.

Cohen D (1981) Broadmoor. London, Psychology News Press.

Confederation of Health Service Employees (1977) The management of violent or potentially violent patients. Banstead, COHSE.

Confederation of Health Service Employees (1979) NHS secure treatment units: a policy statement. Banstead, COHSE.

Curran W J and Harding T W (1978) The law and mental health: harmonizing objectives. Geneva, World Health Organization.

Davies W and Feldman P (1981) The diagnosis of psychopathy by forensic specialists. British Journal of Psychiatry 138: 329–331.

Dell S (1980) The transfer of special hospital patients to NHS hospitals. London, Special Hospitals Research Unit. Report no 16.

Department of Health and Social Security (1971) Better services for the mentally handicapped. Cmnd 4683. London, HMSO.

Department of Health and Social Security (1974) Revised report of the working party on security in NHS psychiatric hospitals (Chairman J Glancy). London, DHSS.

Department of Health and Social Security (1974a) Security in NHS hospitals for the mentally ill and the mentally handicapped. HSC(15)61.

Department of Health and Social Security (1974b) Services for the mentally disordered provided under Section 12 of the Health Services and Public Health Act 1968. LAC(74)19.

Department of Health and Social Security (1975) Better services for the mentally ill. Cmnd 6233. London, HMSO: para 5.2.

Department of Health and Social Security (1975a) Regional security units: design guidelines. London, DHSS.

Department of Health and Social Security (1976) The management of violent, or potentially violent, hospital patients. HC(76)11.

Department of Health and Social Security (1976a) Regional chairmen's enquiry into the working of the DHSS in relation to regional health authorities. London, DHSS: para 217 (e).

Department of Health and Social Security (1978) A review of the Mental Health Act 1959. Cmnd 7320. London, HMSO.

Department of Health and Social Security (1980) Mental handicap: progress, problems and priorities. London, DHSS.

Department of Health and Social Security (1980a) Report of the review of Rampton Hospital (Chairman J Boynton). Cmnd 8073. London, HMSO.

Department of Health and Social Security (1984) Special hospitals patient statistics 1983.

Department of Health and Social Security (1985) Special hospitals patient statistics 1984.

Devlin P (1962) Samples of law making. London, Oxford University Press: 90.

Elliot J (1973) Report on the organisational problems and staff management relationships at Rampton Hospital. Unpublished, summarised in DHSS (1980a) para 3.4.

Elton R (1983) Personal correspondence to Lord Avebury from the Under-Secretary of State at the Home Office.

Faulk M (1979) The Lyndhurst Unit at Knowle Hospital. Bulletin of the Royal College of Psychiatrists, March: 44–46.

Faulk M (1979a) Mentally disordered offenders in an interim regional medium secure unit. Criminal Law Review: 686–695.

Faulk M (1985) Secure facilities in local psychiatric hospitals. In: Gostin L (ed) Secure provision: a review of special services for the mentally ill and mentally handicapped in England and Wales. London, Tavistock Publications: 69–83.

Folkard S (1960) Aggressive behaviour in relation to open wards in a mental hospital. Mental Hygiene 44: 155–161.

Gibbens T C N (1961) Treatment of psychopaths. Journal of Mental Science 107: 181–186.

Gostin L (1977) A Human Condition: the law relating to mentally abnormal offenders. Observations, analysis and proposals for reform. Vol 2. London, MIND.

Gostin L (1978) The right of a mentally handicapped person to a home, to education and to socialisation: a case for exclusion from the Mental Health Act 1959. Apex: Journal of the Institute for Mental Subnormality 6, 2: 28–31.

Gostin L (1979) The law relating to mental handicap in England and Wales. In: Craft M (ed) Tredgold's mental retardation. 12th edition. London, Baillière Tindall: 271–287.

Gostin L (1983) A practical guide to mental health law. London, MIND.

Gostin L (1983a) The ideology of entitlement: the application of contemporary legal approaches to psychiatry. In: Bean P (ed) Mental illness: changes and trends. Chichester, John Wiley & Sons: 27–54.

Gostin L (1985) Mental health services and the law. London, Shaw and Sons.

Gostin L and Staunton M (1985) The case for prison standards: conditions of confinement, segregation and medical treatment. In: McGuire M, Vaag J and Morgan R (eds) Accountability and prisons: opening up a closed world. London, Tavistock Publications.

Gray K C and Hutchison H C (1964) The psychopathic personality: a survey of Canadian psychiatrists' opinions. Canadian Psychiatric Association Journal 9: 452–461.

Guardian, The. 12 November 1980. Minister acts to speed transfers from Rampton.

Guardian, The. February 1985.

Gudjonsson G H and MacKeith J A C (1983) A regional interim secure unit at the Bethlem Royal Hospital – the first fourteen months. Medicine, Science and the Law 23: 209–219.

Gunn J (1979) The law and the mentally abnormal offender in England and Wales. International Journal of Law and Psychiatry 2: 199–214.

Gunn J (1985) Psychiatry and the Prison Medical Service. In: Gostin L (ed) Secure provision: a review of special services for the mentally ill and mentally handicapped in England and Wales. London, Tavistock Publications: 126–152.

Gunn J, Robertson G, Dell S and Way C (1978) Psychiatric aspects of imprisonment. London, Academic Press.

Guze S B (1976) Criminality and psychiatric disorders. New York, Oxford University Press.

Hamilton J (1985) The special hospitals. In: Gostin L (ed) Secure provision: a review of special services for the mentally ill and mentally handicapped in England and Wales. London, Tavistock Publications: 84–125.

Harding T W, Schneider J and Visotsky H (1985) Human rights and the treatment of mental patients in Japan: conclusions and recommendations of an expert mission. Geneva, International Commission of Jurists.

Higgins J (1979) Rainford Ward, Rainhill Hospital, Merseyside. Bulletin of the Royal College of Psychiatrists, March: 43–44.

Higgins J (1981) Four years' experience of an interim secure unit. British Medical Journal 282: 889–893.

Hoggett B (1984) Mental health law. Second edition. London, Sweet and Maxwell.

Hoggett B (1985) Legal aspects of secure provision. In: Gostin L (ed) Secure provision: a review of special services for the mentally ill and mentally handicapped in England and Wales. London, Tavistock Publications: 236–262.

Home Office (1964) Report of the working party on the organisation of the Prison Medical Service (Chairman E H Gwynn). London, HMSO.

Home Office (1974) Interim report of the Committee on Mentally Abnormal Offenders (Chairman Lord Butler). Cmnd 5698. London, HMSO.

Home Office (1975) Report of the Committee on Mentally Abnormal Offenders (Chairman Lord Butler). Cmnd 6244. London, HMSO.

Home Office (1979) Committee of inquiry into the United Kingdom prison services (Chairman Sir John May). Cmnd 7673. London, HMSO.

Home Office (1980) Report on the work of the Prison Department 1979. Cmnd 7965. London, HMSO.

Home Office (1982) Report on the work of the Prison Department 1981. Cmnd 8543. London, HMSO: paras 241–252.

Home Office (1983) Criminal statistics England and Wales 1982. Cmnd 9048. London, HMSO.

House of Commons Estimates Committee (1968) Second report: the special hospitals and the state hospitals. Session 1967–1968. London, HMSO.

Independent Development Council for People with Mental Handicap (1982) Elements of a comprehensive local service for people with mental handicap. London, IDC.

Lanham D (1974) Arresting the insane. Criminal Law Review: 515–528.

Lewis P (1980) Psychiatric probation orders: roles and expectations of probation officers and psychiatrists. Cambridge, Institute of Criminology. Occasional Paper no 6.

McFarlane M A and Wells O (1984) Mental health and the offender: care in the community. National Association of Probation Officers, Social Policy Committee.

McLean E (1975) Prison and humanity. The Lancet I: 507–511.

MIND (1980) Mind Out, November/December.

MIND (1983) Common Concern.

MIND (1985) Open Mind, February/March.

Ministry of Health (1959) Mental health services. HM(59)46.

Ministry of Health (1961) Treatment of psychiatric patients under security conditions. HM(61)69.

Ministry of Health (1961a) Special hospitals: report of a working party. London, HMSO.

Montandon C and Harding T W (1984) The reliability of dangerousness assessments. British Journal of Psychiatry 144: 149–155.

Moerloose J (1961) Compulsory or voluntary vaccination. In: The role of immunisation in communicable diseases control. Geneva, World Health Organization. Public Health Papers 8: 85–100.

Newton M (1971) Reconviction after treatment at Grendon. London, Home Office, Prison Department, Office of the Chief Psychologist. CP report, series B, no 1.

NHS Hospital Advisory Service (1971) Report on Rampton Hospital. Unpublished, summarised in DHSS (1980a): para 3.3.

NHS Hospital Advisory Service (1975) Report on Broadmoor Hospital. Unpublished.

Orr J (1978) The imprisonment of mentally disordered offenders. British Journal of Psychiatry 133: 194–199.

Oxford University. Department of Psychiatry (1976) A survey of the need for secure psychiatric facilities in the Oxford region. Oxford RHA.

Oxford University. Department of Psychiatry (1978) A survey of the need for secure psychiatric facilities in the Oxford region: continuation of research. Oxford RHA.

Parliamentary All-Party Mental Health Group (1980) Visit to Broadmoor.

Parliamentary All-Party Penal Affairs Group (1980) Too many prisoners. Chichester, Barry Rose.

Parliamentary All-Party Penal Affairs Group (1982) Summary of points made by Lord Belstead, Lord Elton and officials at a meeting held on 17 March 1982.

Parliamentary debates (1982) House of Lords, vol 431, 16 June. Written answers col 625.

Parliamentary debates (1982a) House of Commons, vol 33, 6 December. Written answers cols 339–340.

Parliamentary debates (1982b) House of Commons, vol 33, 6 December. Written answers cols 390–396.

Parliamentary debates (1983) House of Lords, vol 442, 6 May, cols 271–272.

Parliamentary debates (1984) House of Commons, vol 33, 7 March. Written answers cols 618–619.

Parliamentary debates (1984a) House of Commons, vol 64, 23 July. Written answers cols 412–437.

Parliamentary debates (1984b) House of Commons, vol 64, 23 July. Written answers cols 421–428.

Parliamentary debates (1984c) House of Commons, vol 64, 23 July. Written answers col 438.

Partridge R (1953) Broadmoor: a history of criminal lunacy and its problems. London, Chatto & Windus.

Quinsey V L and Ambtman R (1979) Variables affecting psychiatrists' and teachers' assessments of dangerousness of mentally ill offenders. Journal of Consulting and Clinical Psychology 47: 353–362.

Rampton Review Board (1982) First Annual Report to the Secretary of State for Social Services.

Rampton Review Board (1983) Second Annual Report to the Secretary of State for Social Services.

Reid A, Lea J and Wallace D (1982) Rehabilitation in Elton Ward, an interim regional secure unit. Nursing Times 78, occasional papers: 29–32.

Roth L H (1980) Correctional psychiatry. In: Curran W J, McGarry A L and Petty C S (eds) Modern legal medicine, psychiatry and forensic science. Philadelphia, F A Davis.

Royal College of Psychiatrists (1979) The College's evidence to the prison services inquiry. Bulletin of the Royal College of Psychiatrists, May: 81–84.

Royal Commission on the Law Relating to Mental Illness and Mental Deficiency (1957) Report (Chairman Lord Percy). Cmnd 169. London, HMSO.

Scott P D (1975) Has psychiatry failed in the treatment of offenders? London, ISTD. Fifth Denis Carroll Memorial Lecture.

Snowden P (1983) The regional secure units programme: a personal appraisal. Bulletin of the Royal College of Psychiatrists 7: 138–140.

South East Thames Regional Health Authority (1979) Secure but not secured. Second (revised) edition. Croydon, SETRHA.

Steadman H J (1983) Predicting dangerousness among the mentally ill: art, magic, science. International Journal of Law and Psychiatry 6: 381–390.

Stern E S (1957) Operation Sesame. The Lancet I: 577–578.

Stone A A (1975) Mental health and the law: a system in transition. Rockville (Md), National Institute for Mental Health.

Street D R K and Tong J E (1960) Rampton – a special hospital. The Lancet II: 143–145.

Stuart and Shine (1984) Report on Holloway Prison C–1 unit. Unpublished.

Sturt E, Wykes T and Creer C (1982) A survey of long-term users of the community psychiatric services in Camberwell. Psychological Medicine monograph supplement 2, part 1: 5–55.

Trautman J R (1984) A brief history of Hansen's disease. Bulletin of the New York Academy of Medicine 60: 689–695.

Treasaden I H (1985) Current practice in regional interim secure units. In: Gostin L (ed) Secure provision: a review of special services for the mentally ill and mentally handicapped in England and Wales. London, Tavistock Publications: 176–207.

Trent Regional Health Authority and Central Nottinghamshire Health Authority (1982) Report of a joint sub-committee to review the working of the Eastdale Unit, Balderton Hospital. Sheffield, Trent RHA.

Woodside M and others (1976) An experiment in managing sociopathic behaviour disorders. British Medical Journal 2: 1056–1059.

Wykes T, Creer C and Sturt E (1982) Needs and the deployment of services. Psychological Medicine monograph supplement 2, part 1: 41–55.

Zusman J and Simon J (1983) Differences in repeated psychiatric examinations of litigants to a lawsuit. American Journal of Psychiatry 140: 1300–1304.

CASES

A v the United Kingdom, application no 6840/74. Report of the European Commission of Human Rights adopted on 16 July 1980.

Albert v Lavin (1981) 3 All ER 878.

Ashingdane v Secretary of State for Social Services and others, unpublished, Court of Appeal, 18 February 1980. See *Ashingdane v the United Kingdom*. Report of the European Commission of Human Rights, 12 May 1983.

Ashingdane v the United Kingdom, judgment of the European Court of Human Rights, 28 May 1985.

Attorney-General's Reference (No 6 of 1980) (1981) 73 Cr. App. R. 63.

B v the United Kingdom. European Commission of Human Rights, application no 6870/75. Report of the Commission adopted on 7 October 1981. See particulary dissenting opinions, pages 56–65. See also decision of the Commission as to admissability, 7 May 1981.

Brookshaw v Hopkins (1790) Lofft. 235, at 244.

Brown v the United States 256 US 335 at 343

Buckland v Buckland (1967) 2 All ER 300.

Fletcher v Fletcher (1859) 1 El. & El. 420.

Freeman v Home Office (1984) 1 All ER 1036.

Herring v Boyle (1834) 1 Cr. M. & R. 377.

Home Office v Dorset Yacht Co Ltd (1970) 2 All ER 294.

Kaimowitz v Michigan (1973) 42 USLW 2063.

Meering v Graham-White Aviation Co (1919) 122 TLR 44, at 53–54.

Pountney v Griffiths (1975) 2 All ER 881.

R v Arant The Times, 6 December 1975.

R v Arrowsmith (1976) Criminal Law Review 636.

R v Brazil The Times, 29 October 1975.

R v Clarke (1975) 61 Cr. App. R. 320.

R v Cox (1968) 1 All ER 386.

R v Farrell The Times, 30 January 1976.

R v Fisher (1981) 3 Cr. App. R. (S) 112.

R v Gordon (1981) 3 Cr. App. R. (S) 352.

R v Gouws (1981) 3 Cr. App. R. (S) 325.

R v Harding The Times, 15 June 1983.

R v Hayes (1974) reported in Thomas D A, Current Sentencing Practice; para Fl.2(a).

R v Higginbotham (1961) 3 All ER 616.

R v Holmes (1979) Criminal Law Review 52. Bodmin Crown Court.

R v Howell (1981) 73 Cr. App. R. 31, CA.

R v Julien (1969) 2 All ER 856.

R v Keegan (1982) Justice of the Peace, 6 November: page 695.

R v Ledger The Guardian, 5 and 23 June 1976.

R v Marsden (1968) 2 All ER 341.

R v Morris (1961) 2 All ER 672.

R v Nicholls Not reported. Judgment given 16 April 1973.

R v Officer The Times, 20 February 1976.

R v Runighian (1977) Criminal Law Review 361.

R v Ryan, The Guardian, 15 June 1975.

R v Scanlon (1979) 1 Cr. App. R. (S) 60.

R v Skelton (1983) Criminal Law Review 686.

R v Slater (1979) 1 Cr. App. R. (S) 349.

R v Smith The Guardian, 14 January 1976.

R v Suchodolski The Times, 9 December 1975.

R v Tolley (1978) 68 Cr. App. R. 323.

R v Twigger The Times, 7 February 1976.

R v Walsh (1981) 3 Cr. App. R. (S) 359.

Richardson v LCC (1957) 1 WLR 751, at 761.

Scott v Wakem (1862) 3 F. & F. 327.

Sidaway v Bethlem Royal Hospital Governors and others (1984) 1 All ER 1018.

Sinclair v Broughton (1882) 47 LJ 170.

Symm v Fraser (1863) 3 F. & F. 859.

Townley v Rushworth (1964) 62 LGR 95.

SUBJECT INDEX

Note: Committees and royal commissions are entered under their individual subjects. Legal cases are listed under that heading.

174

NAME INDEX

Note: Names of those involved in legal cases are filed in the subject index under that heading.